MAJESTIC ANIMALS
Coloring Book for Adults

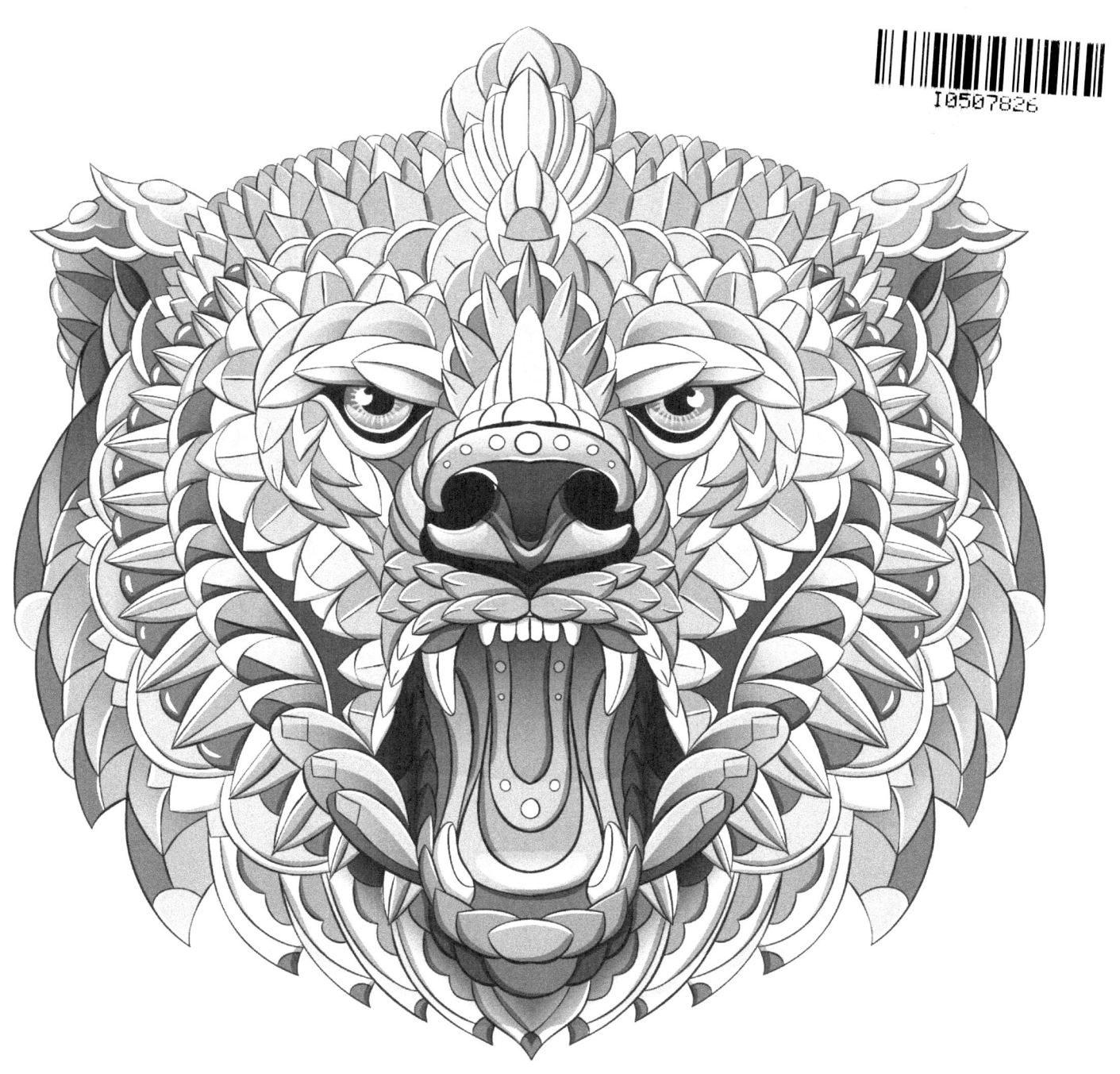

50 Relaxing Designs

Copyright 2020 © Adult Coloring Fun

All rights reserved

No part of this book may be reproduce or used in any form without the written consent of the author and publisher.

Color Test

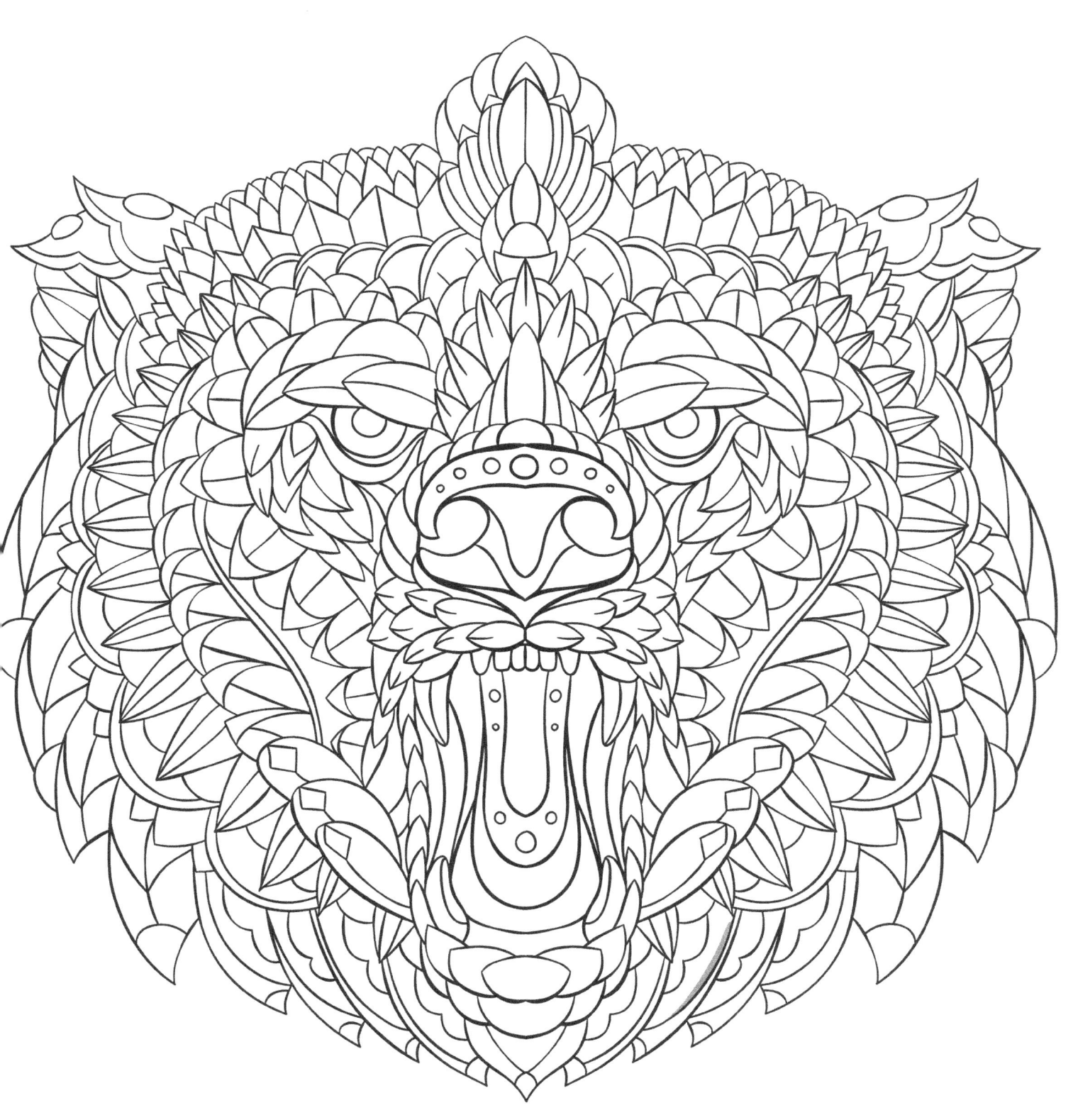

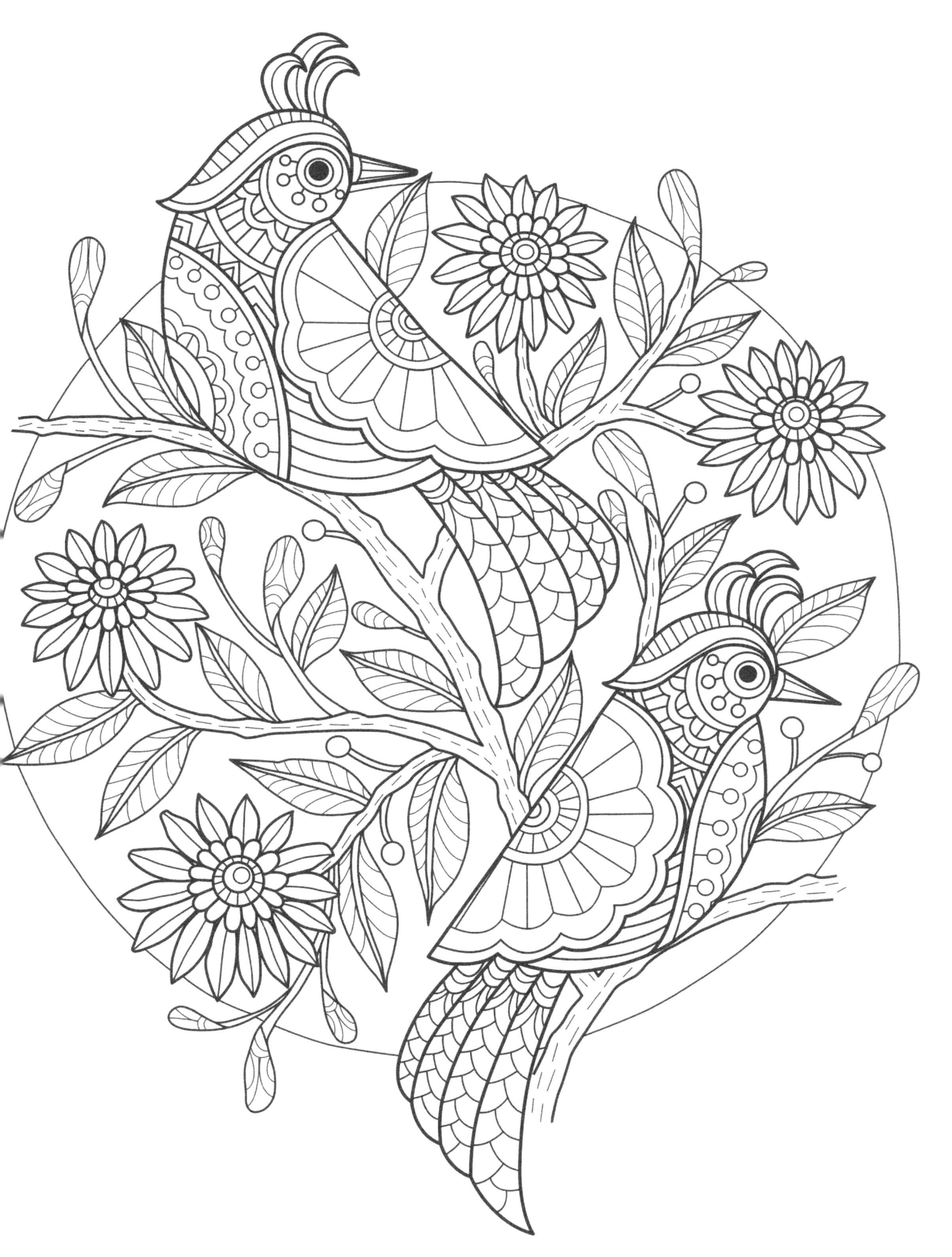

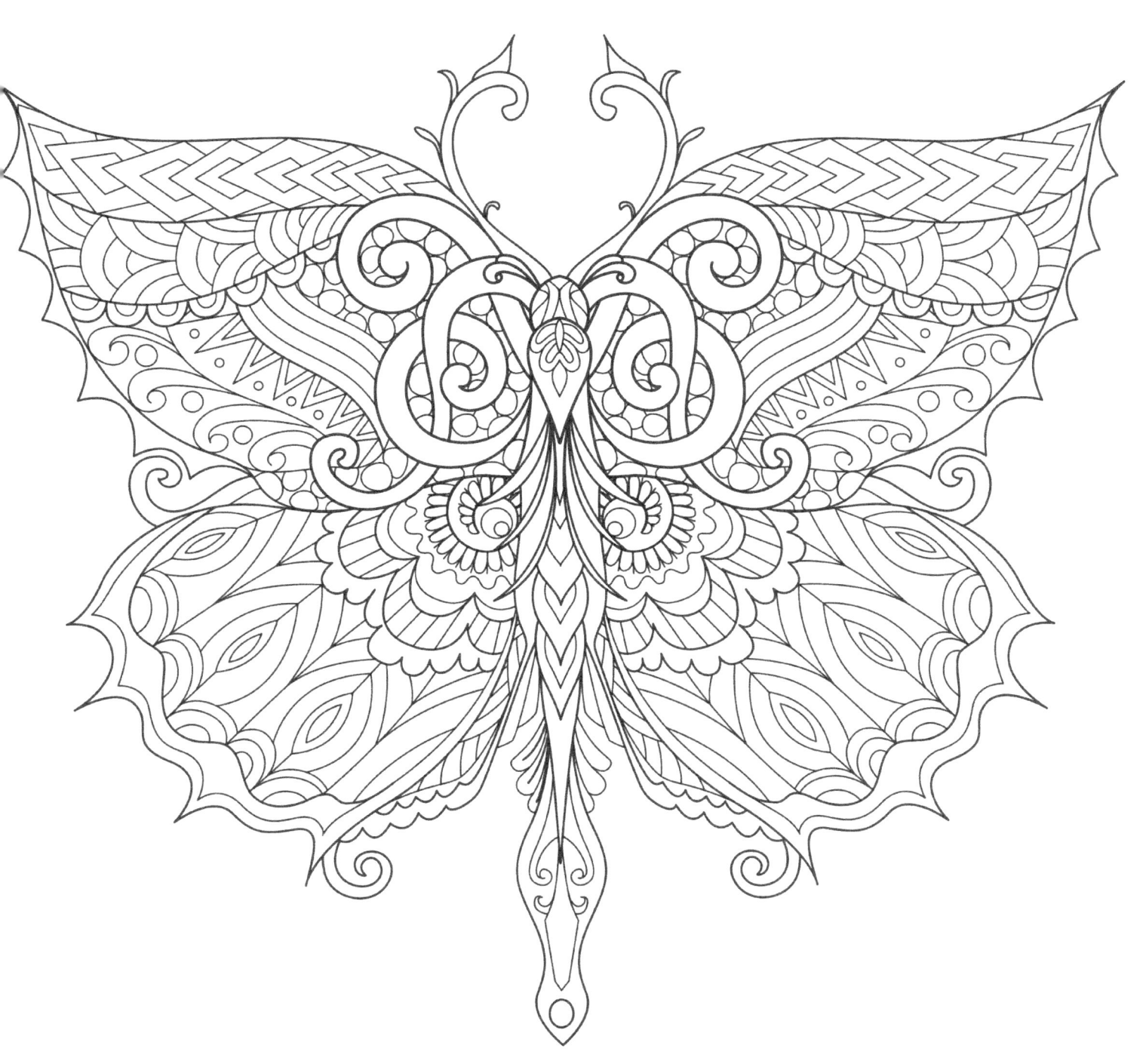

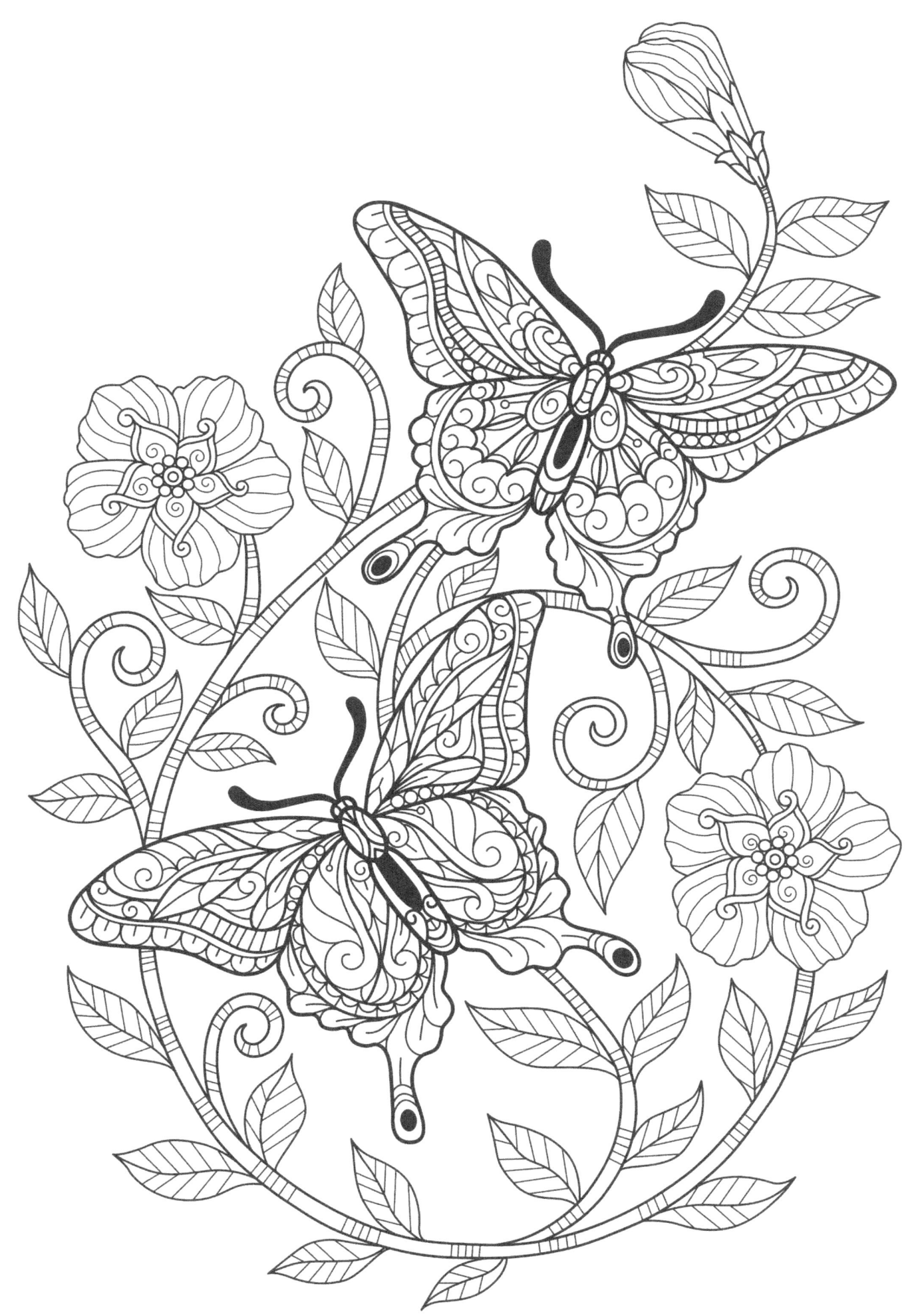

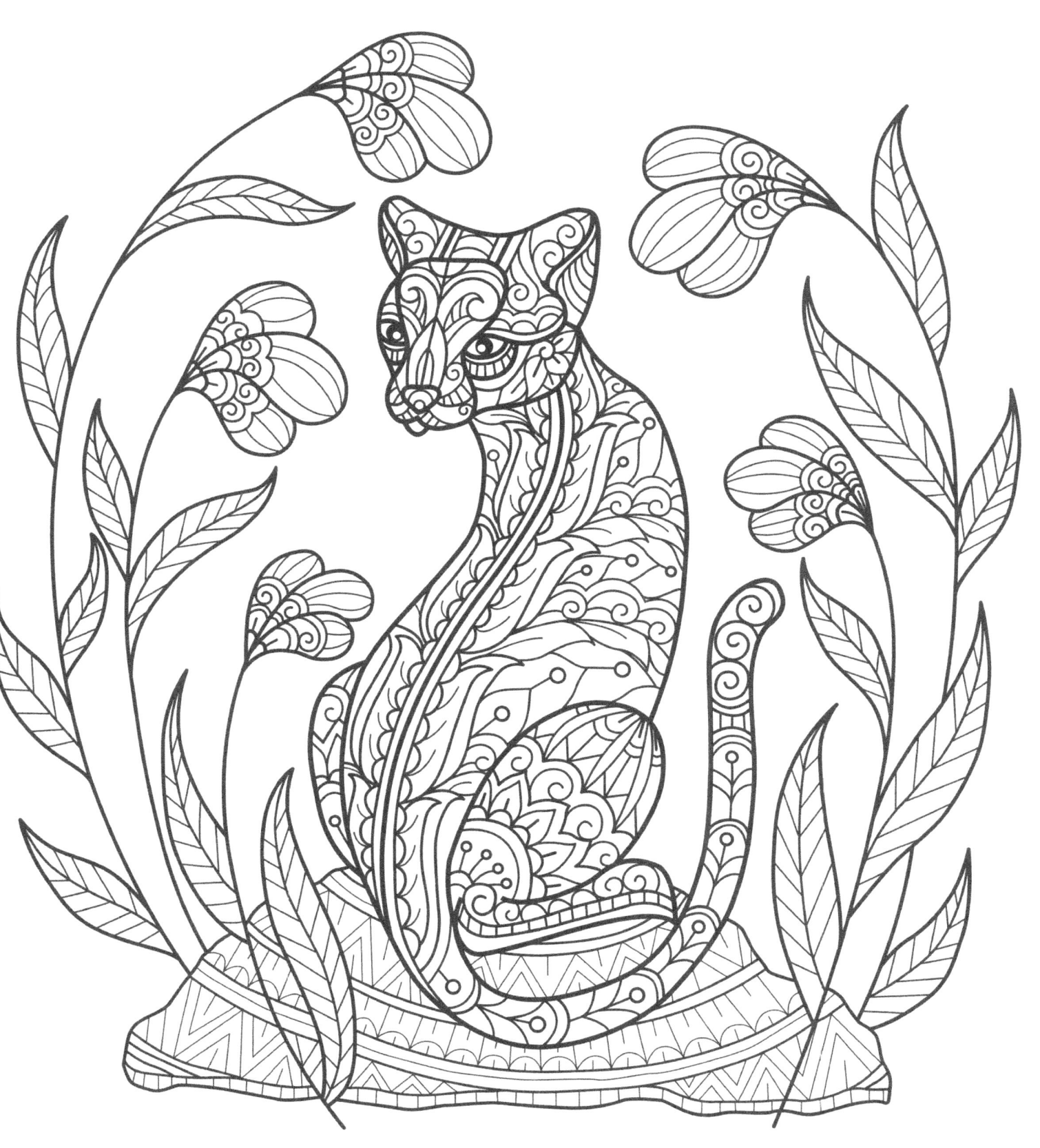

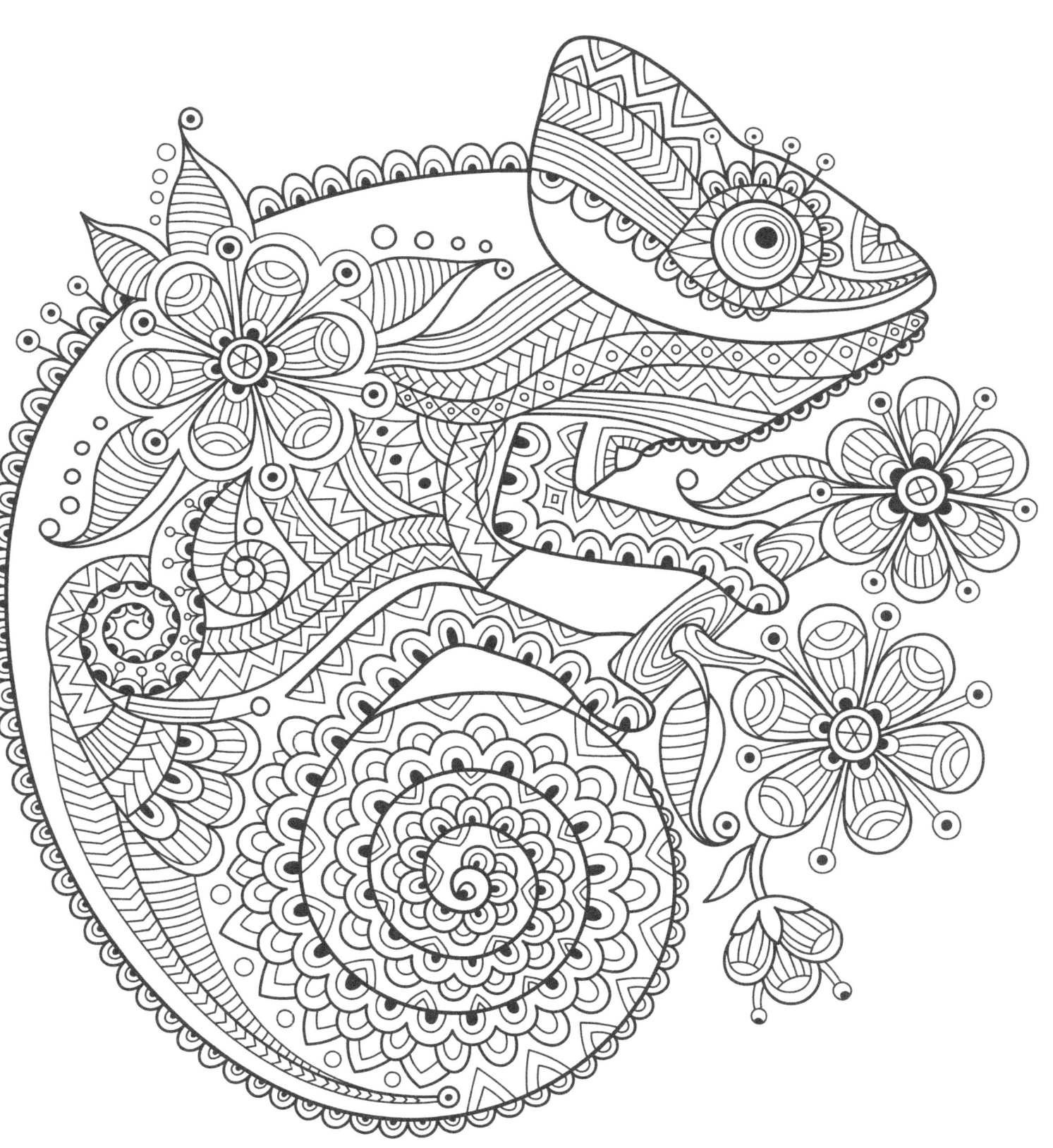

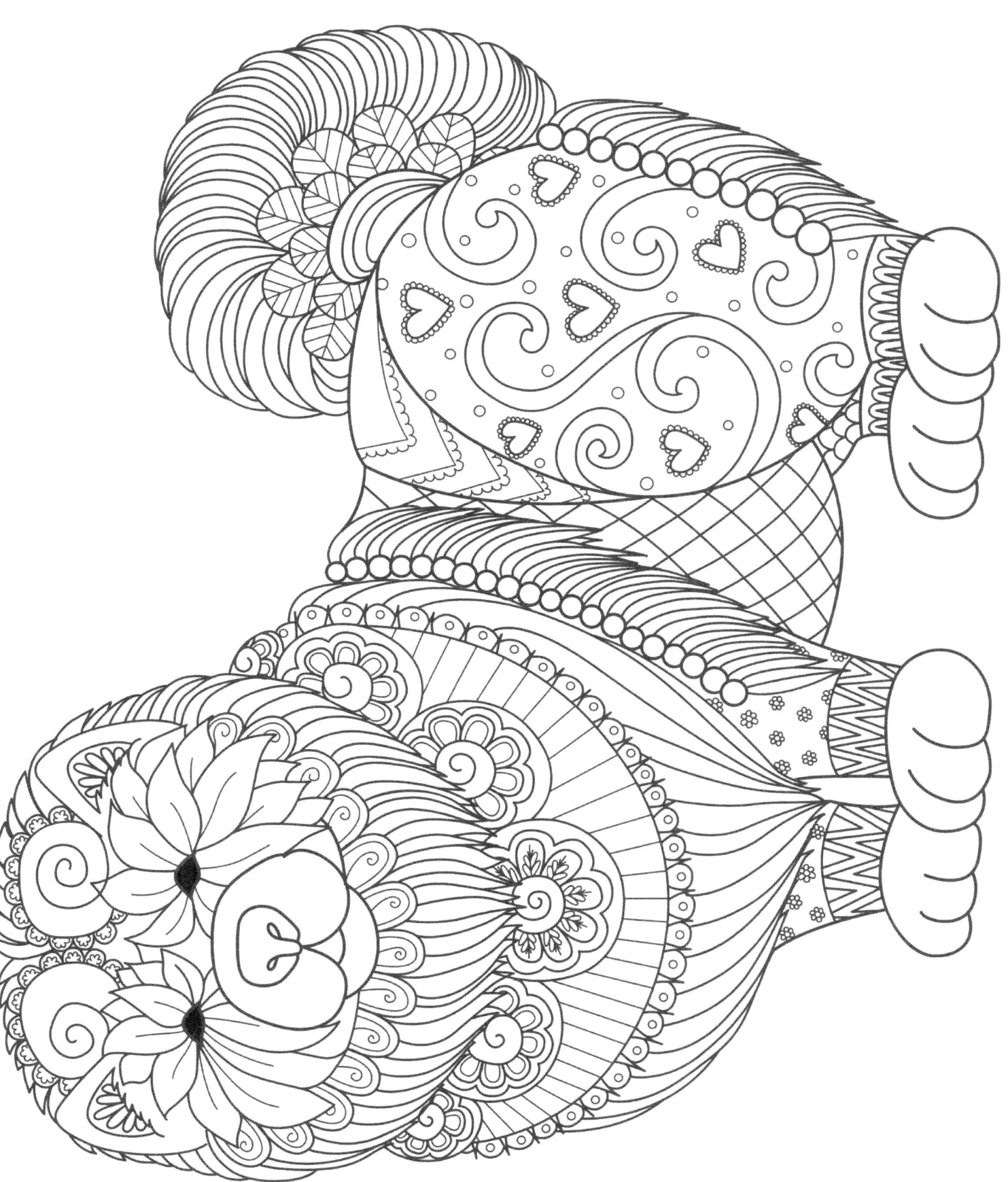

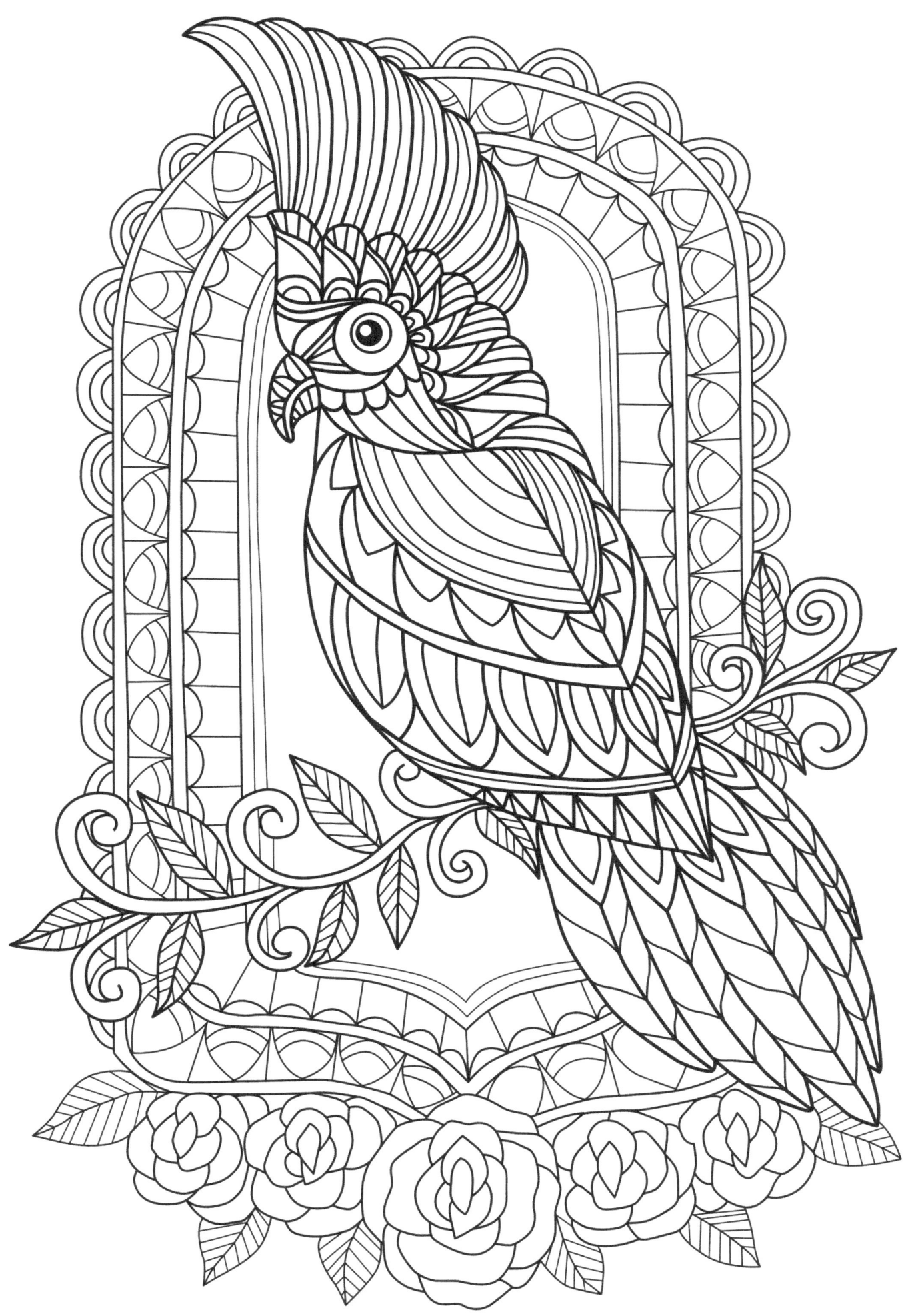

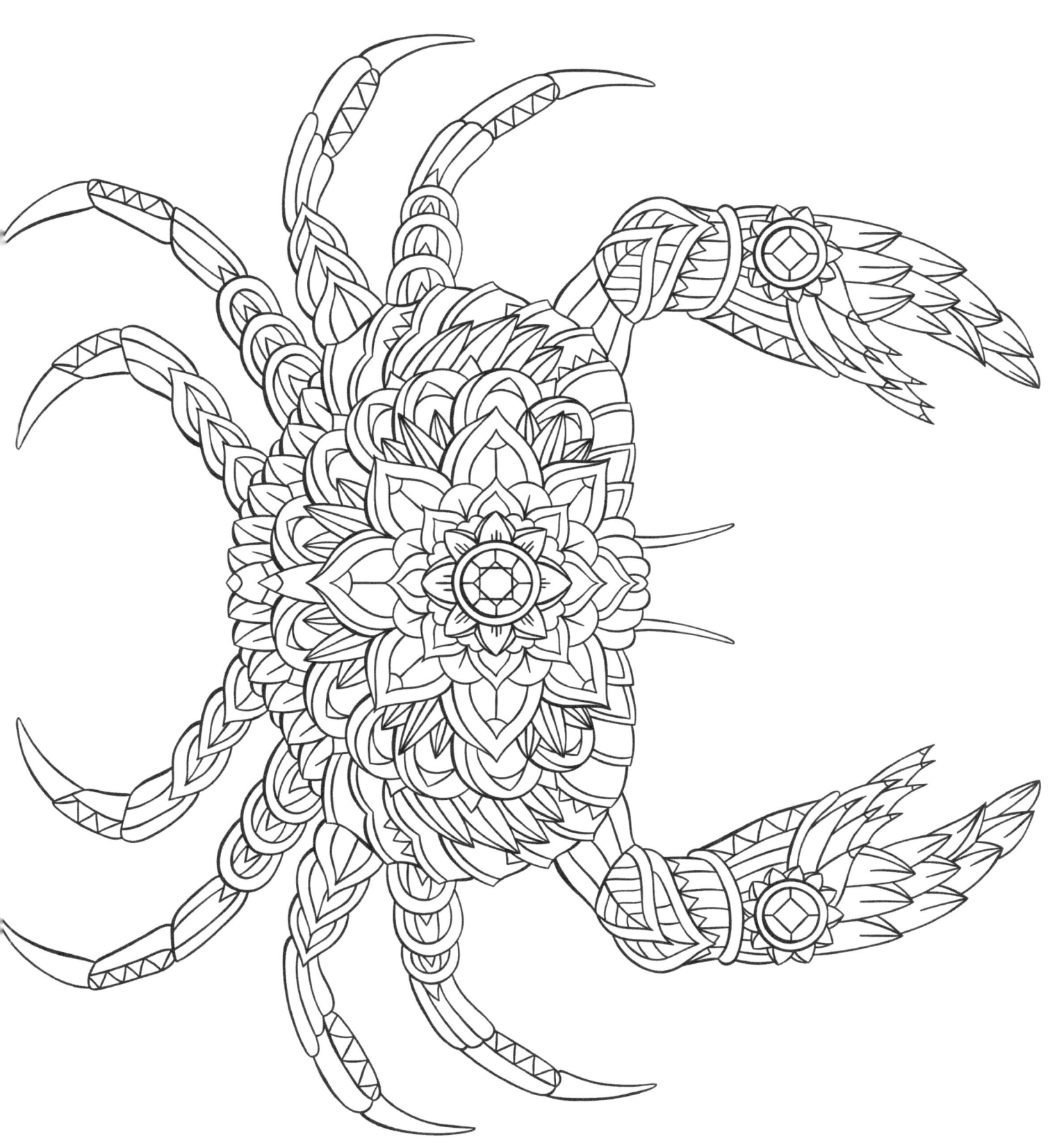

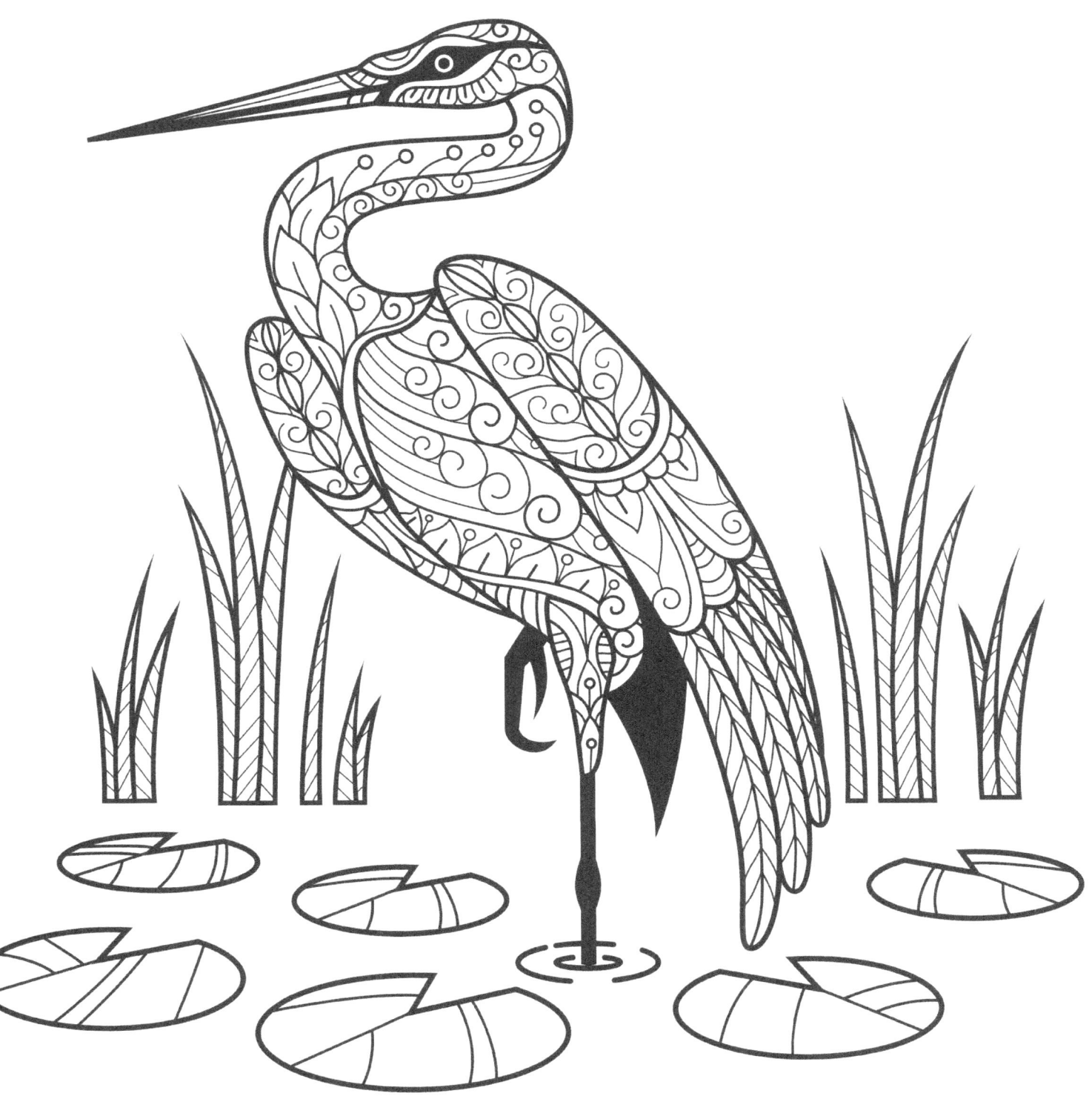

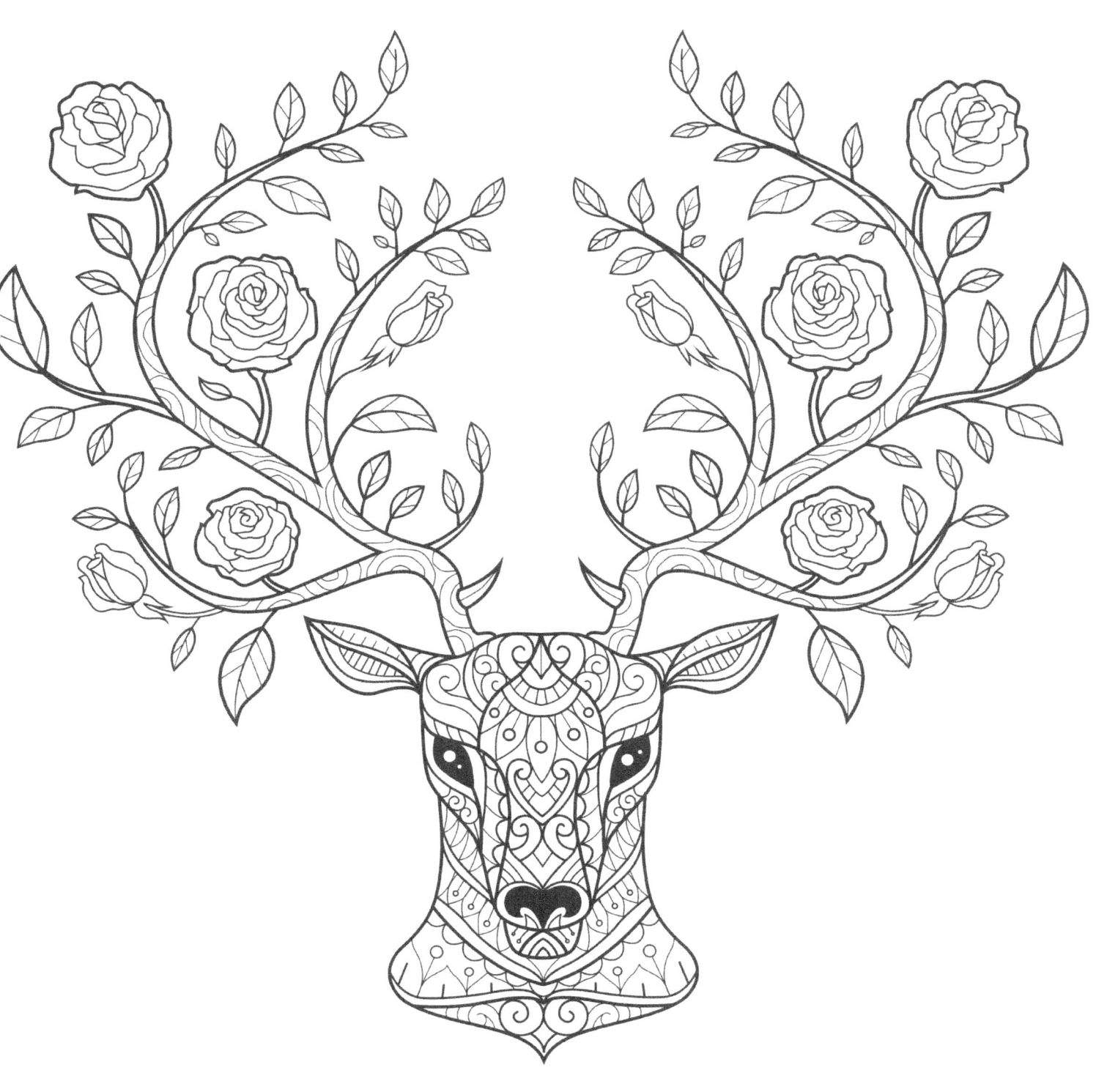

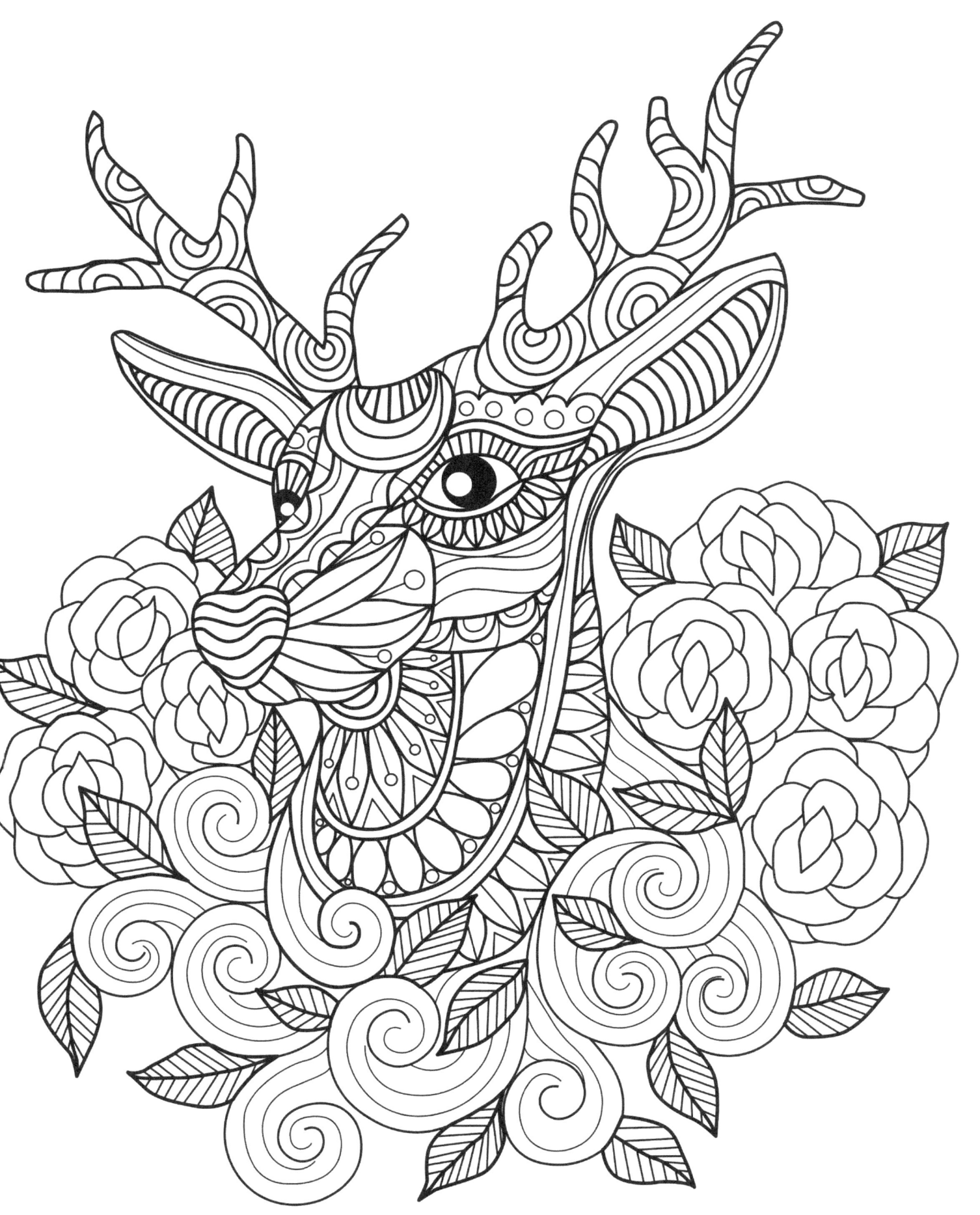

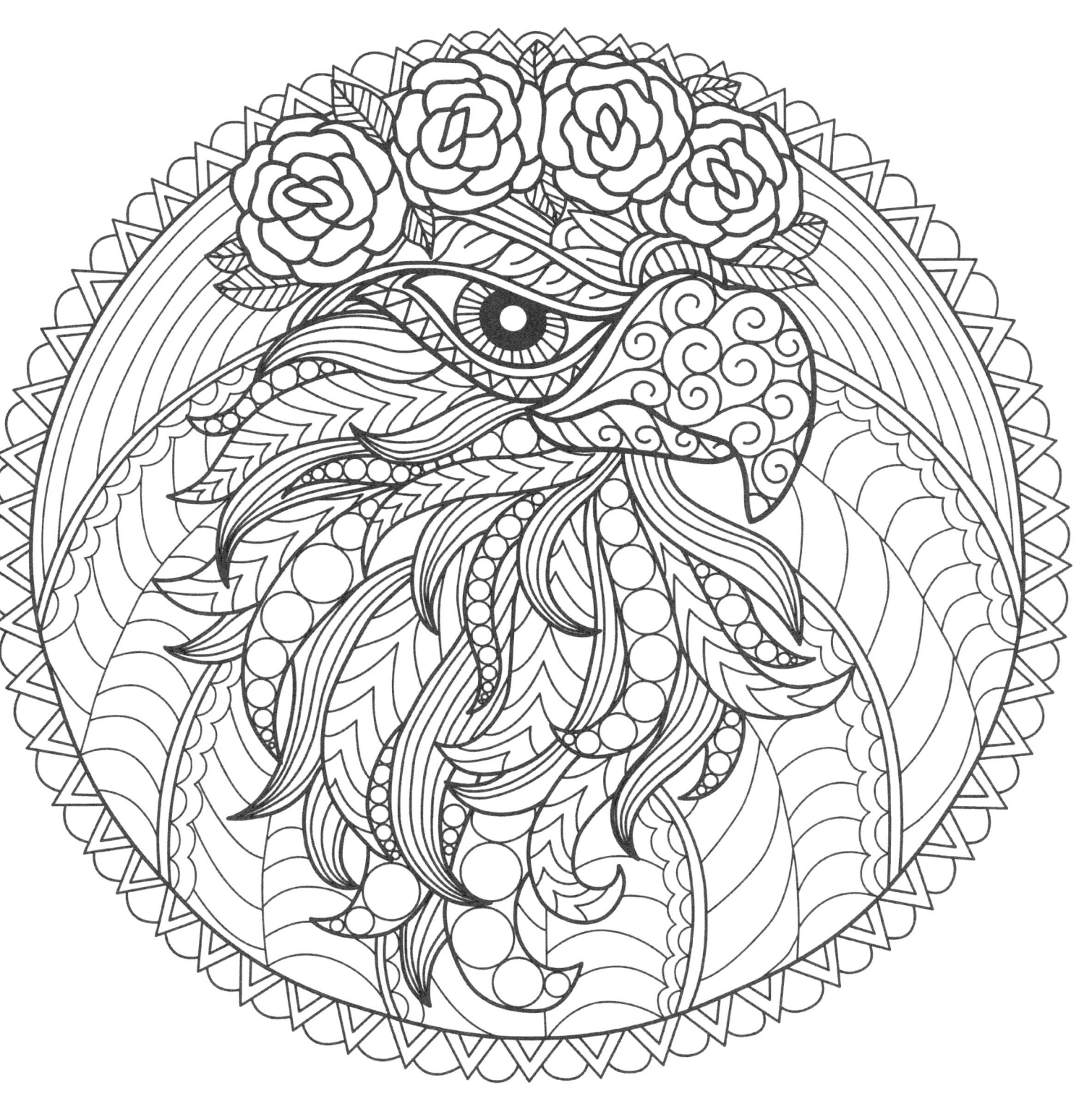

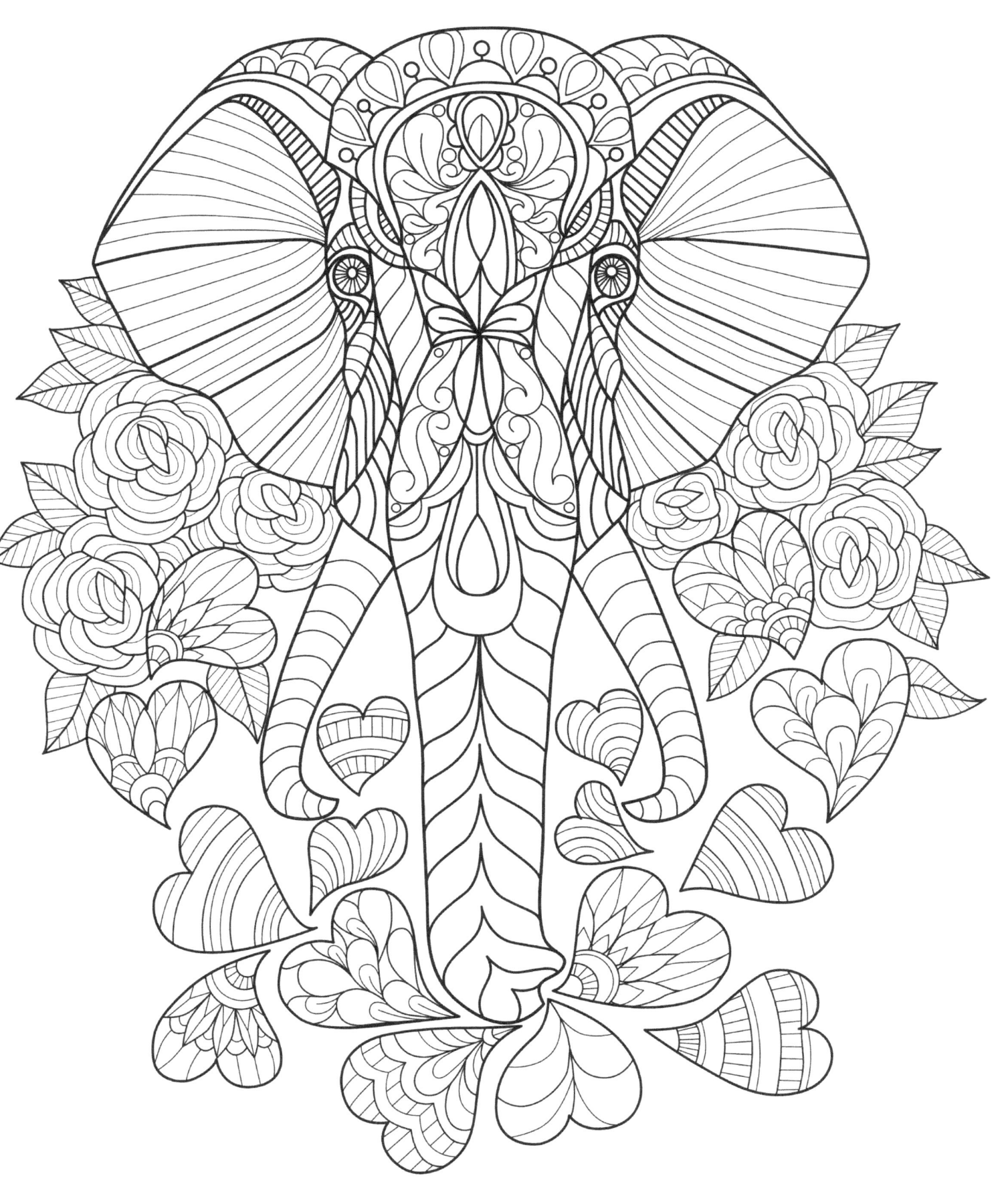

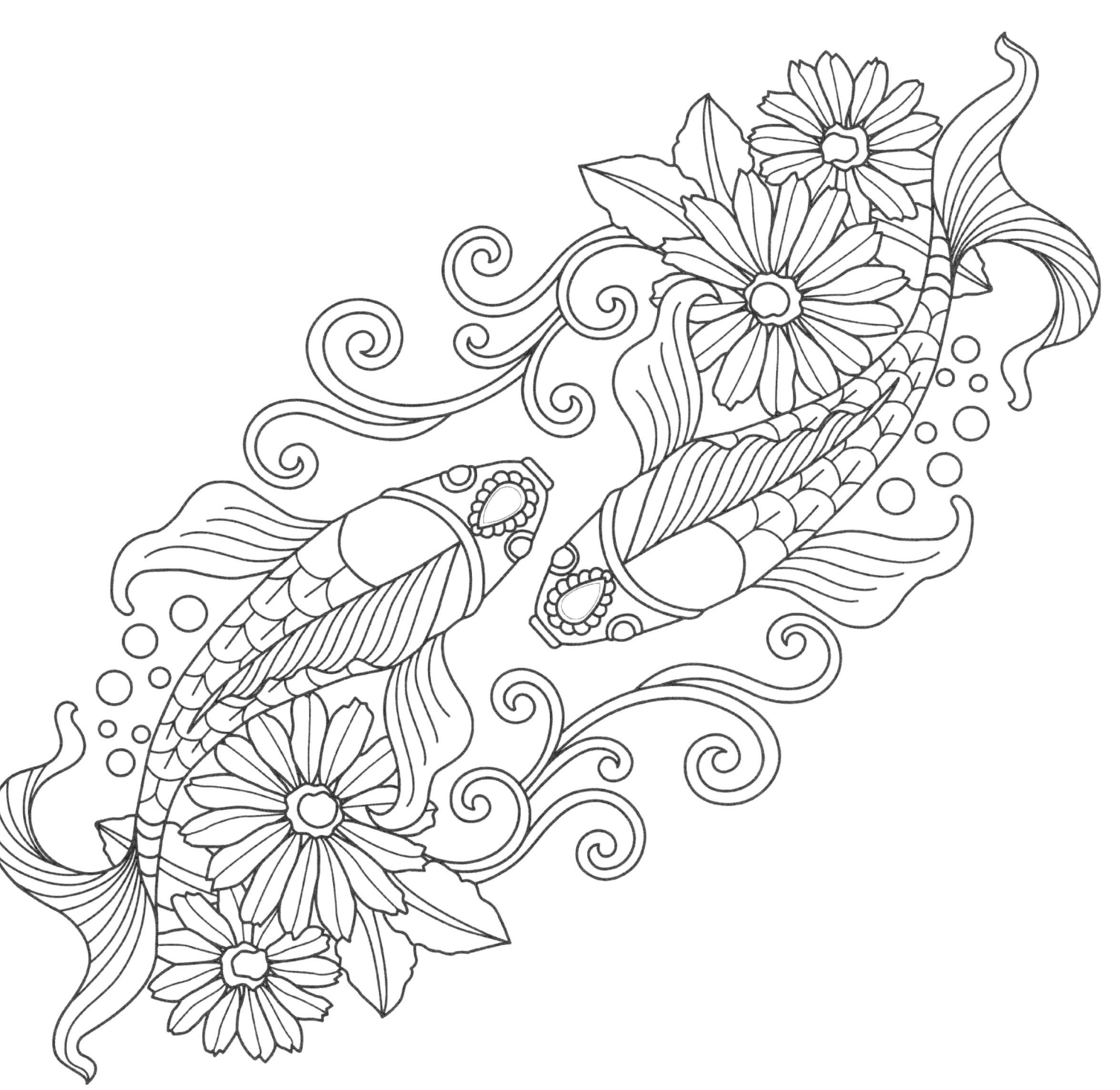

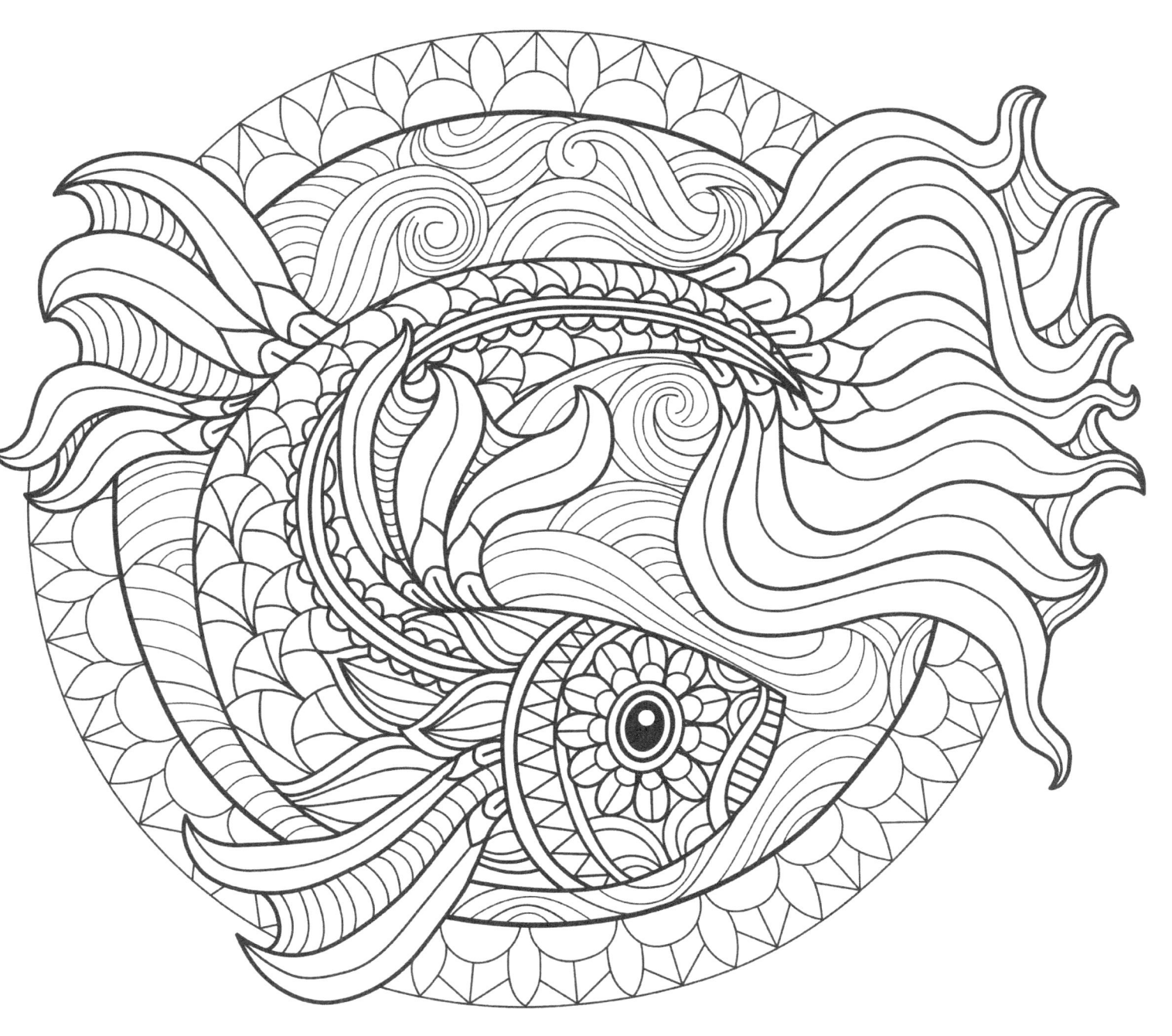

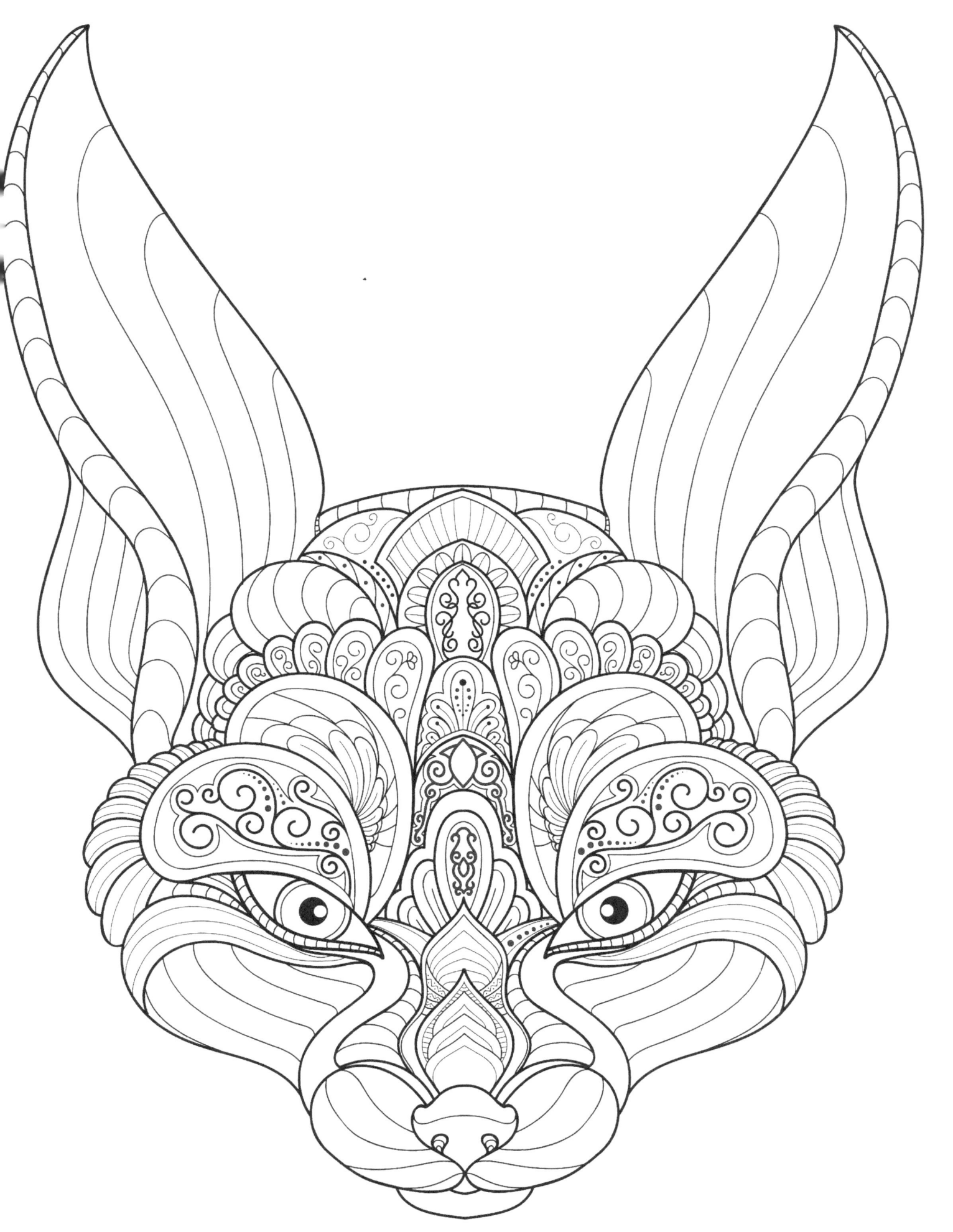

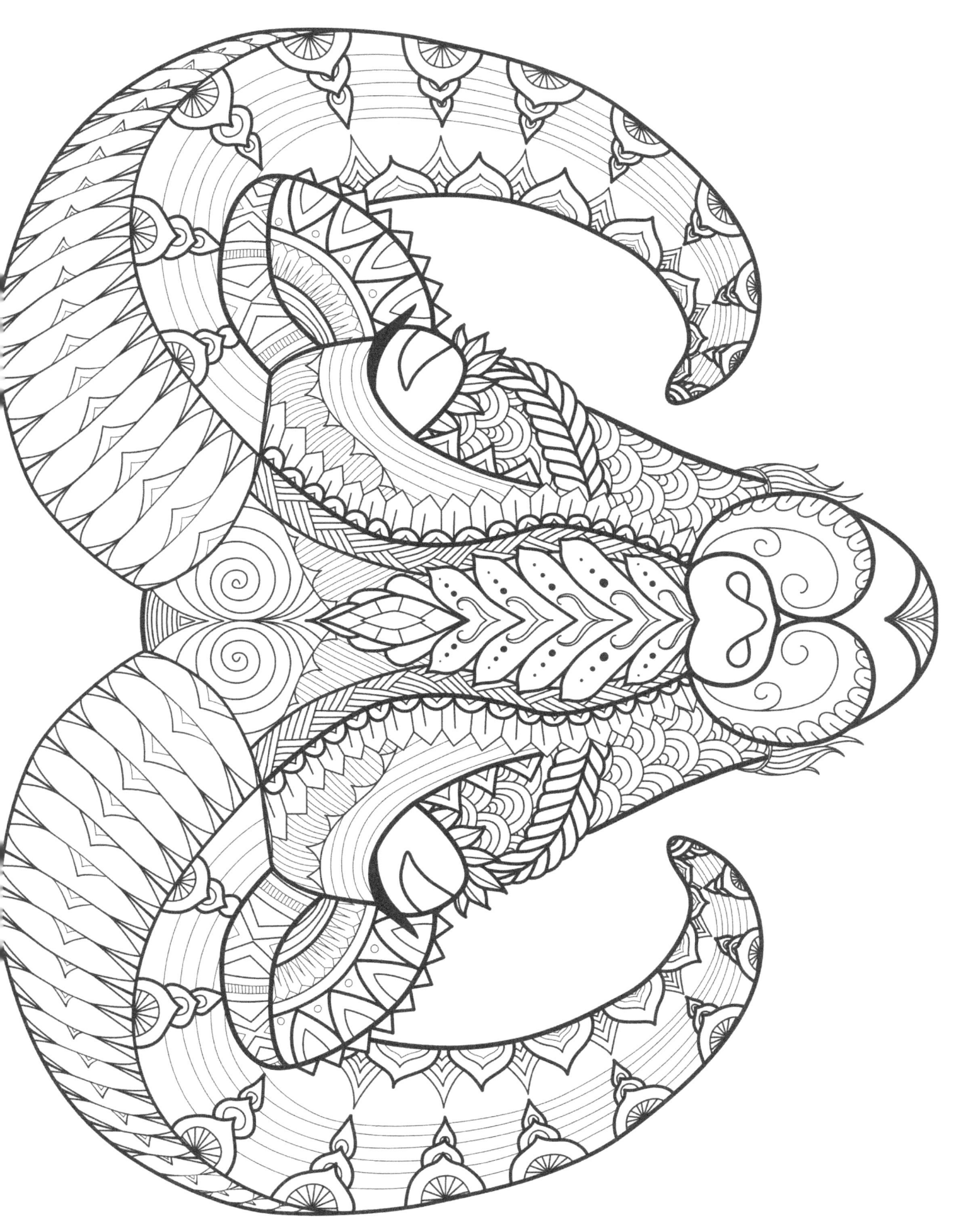

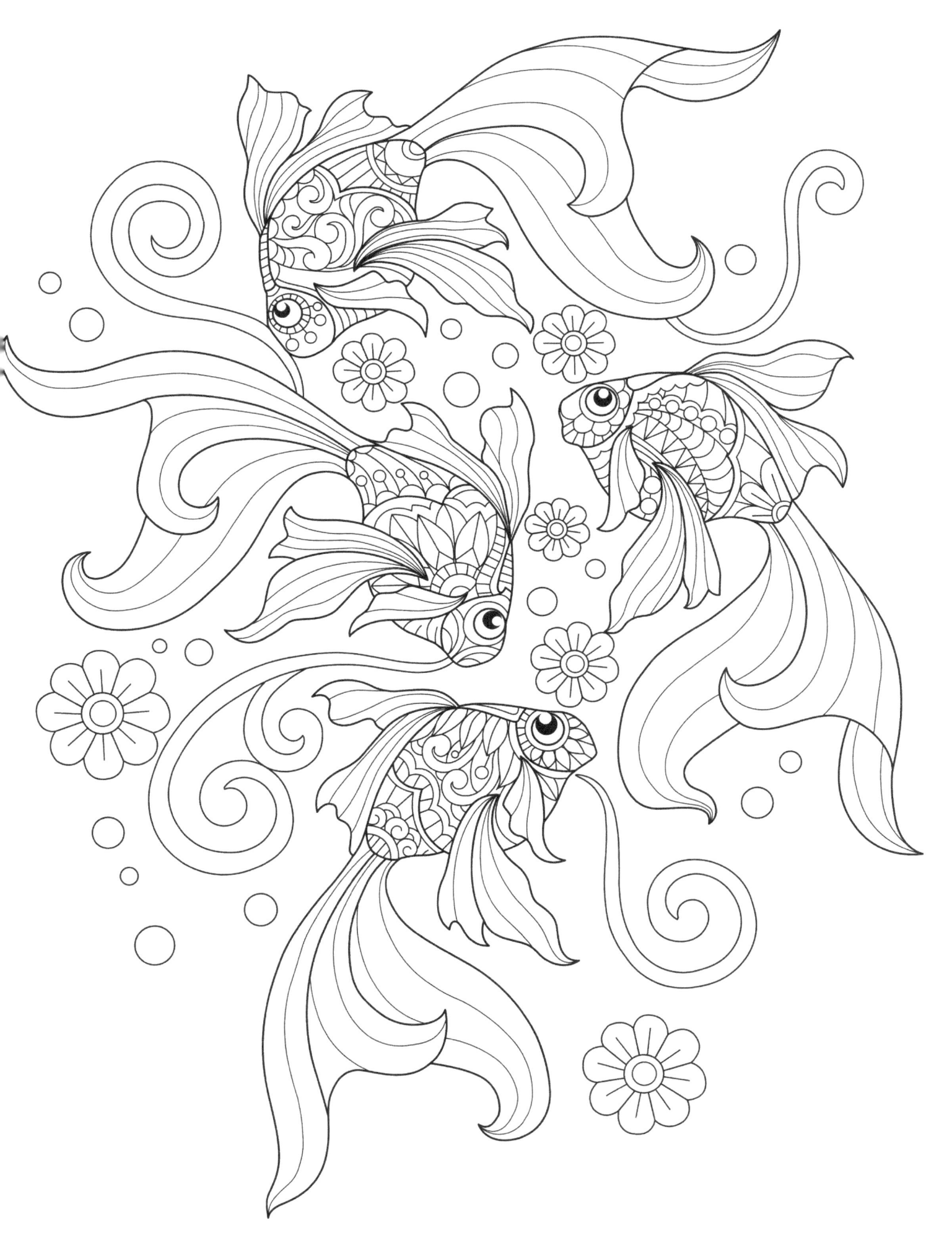

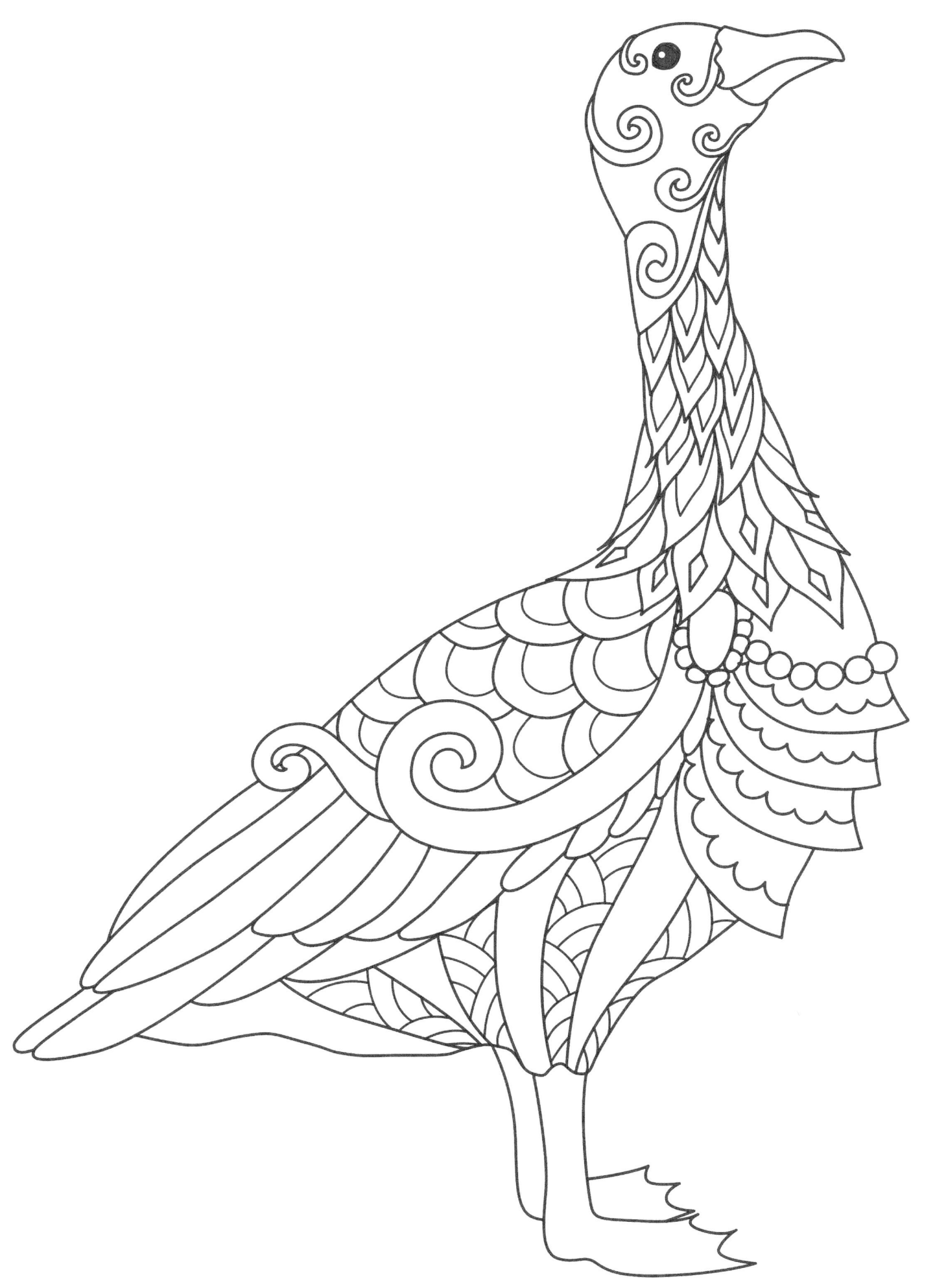

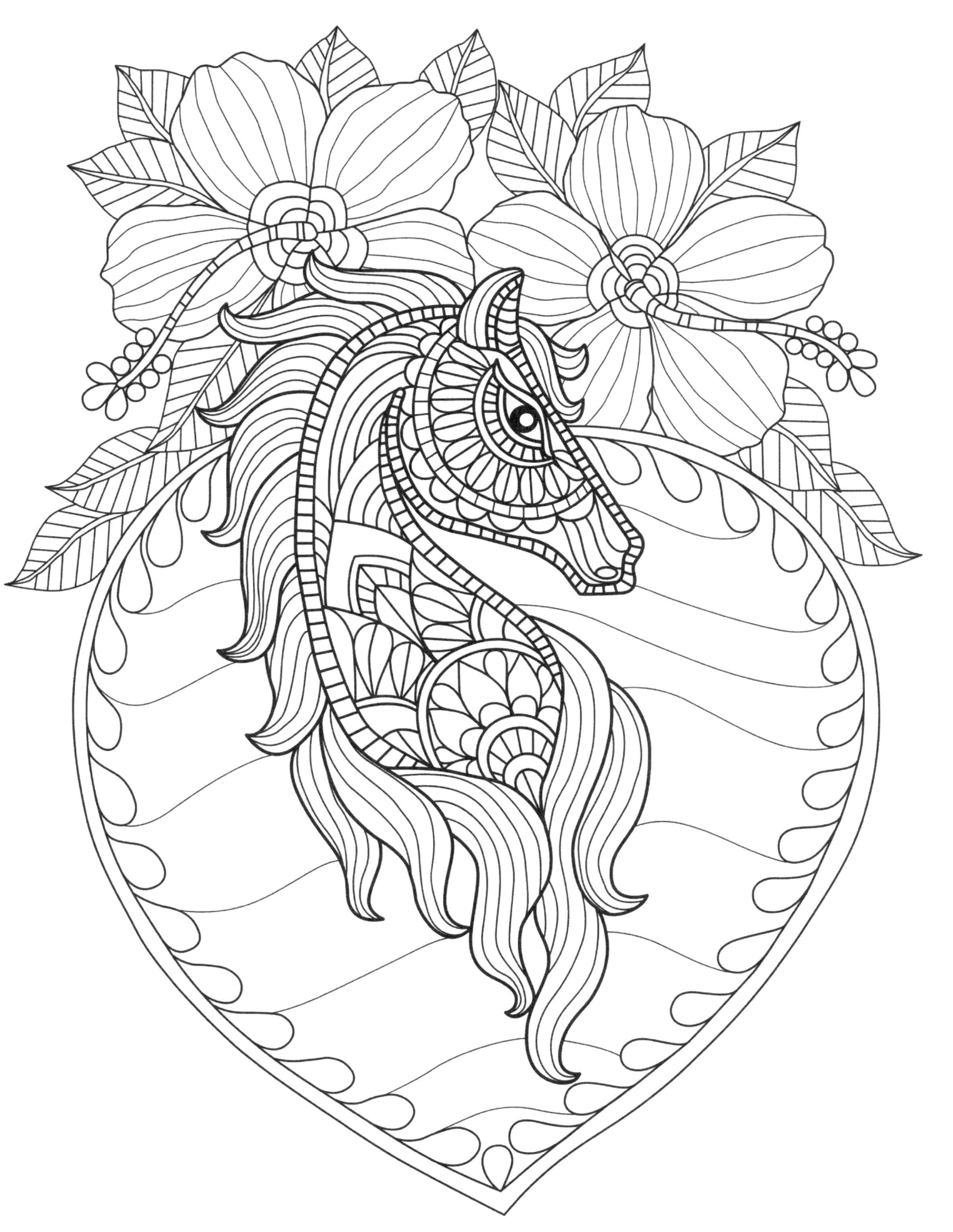

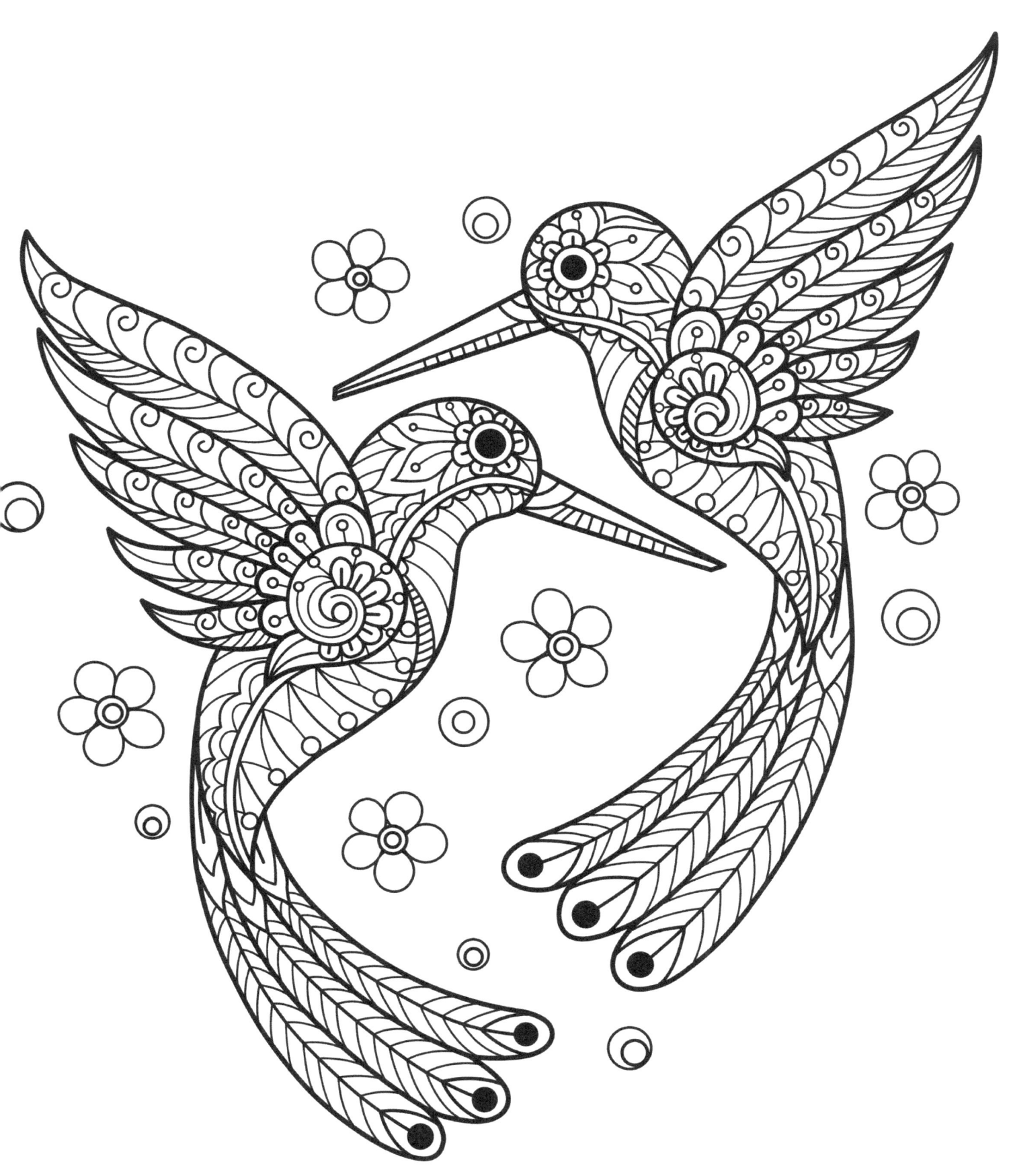

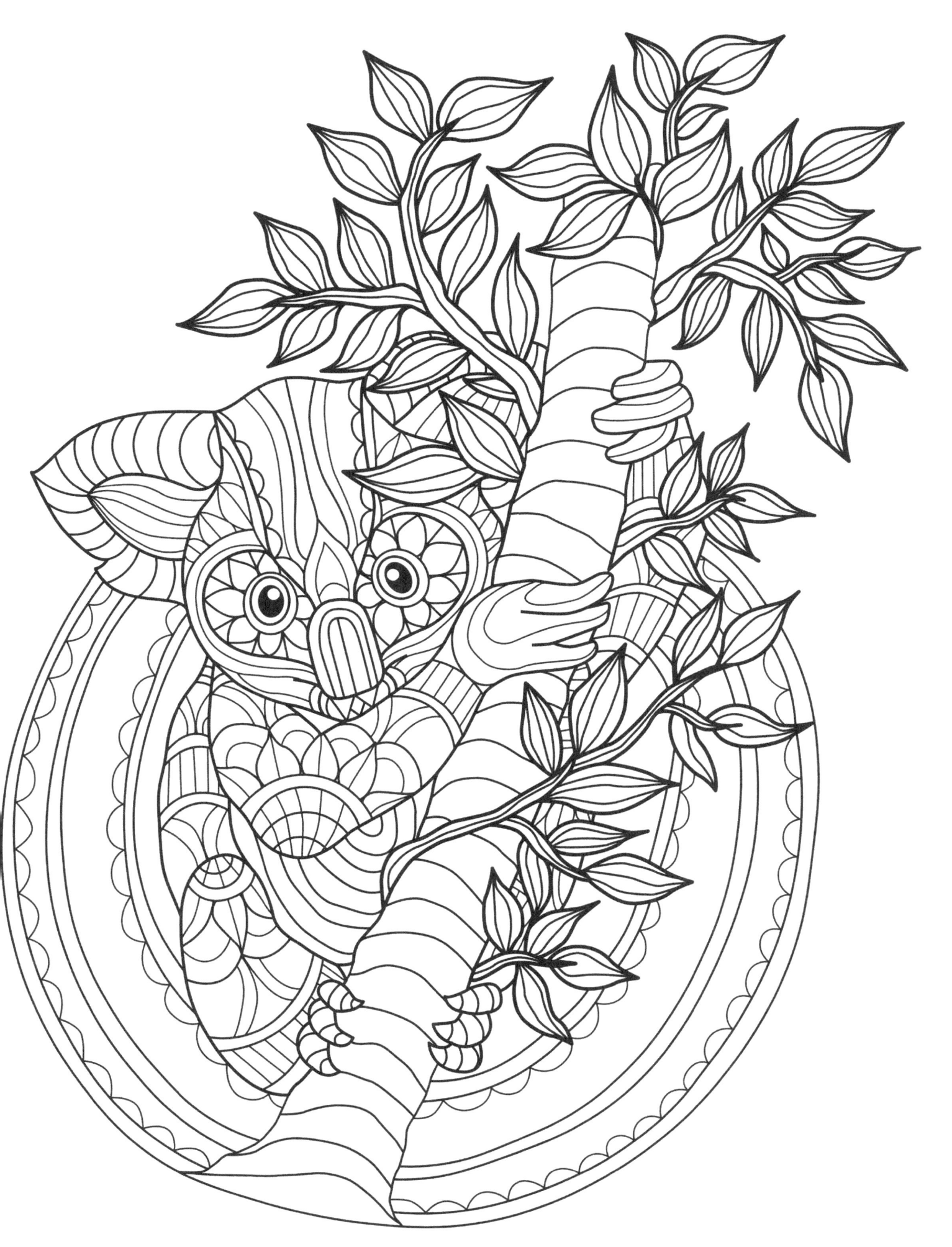

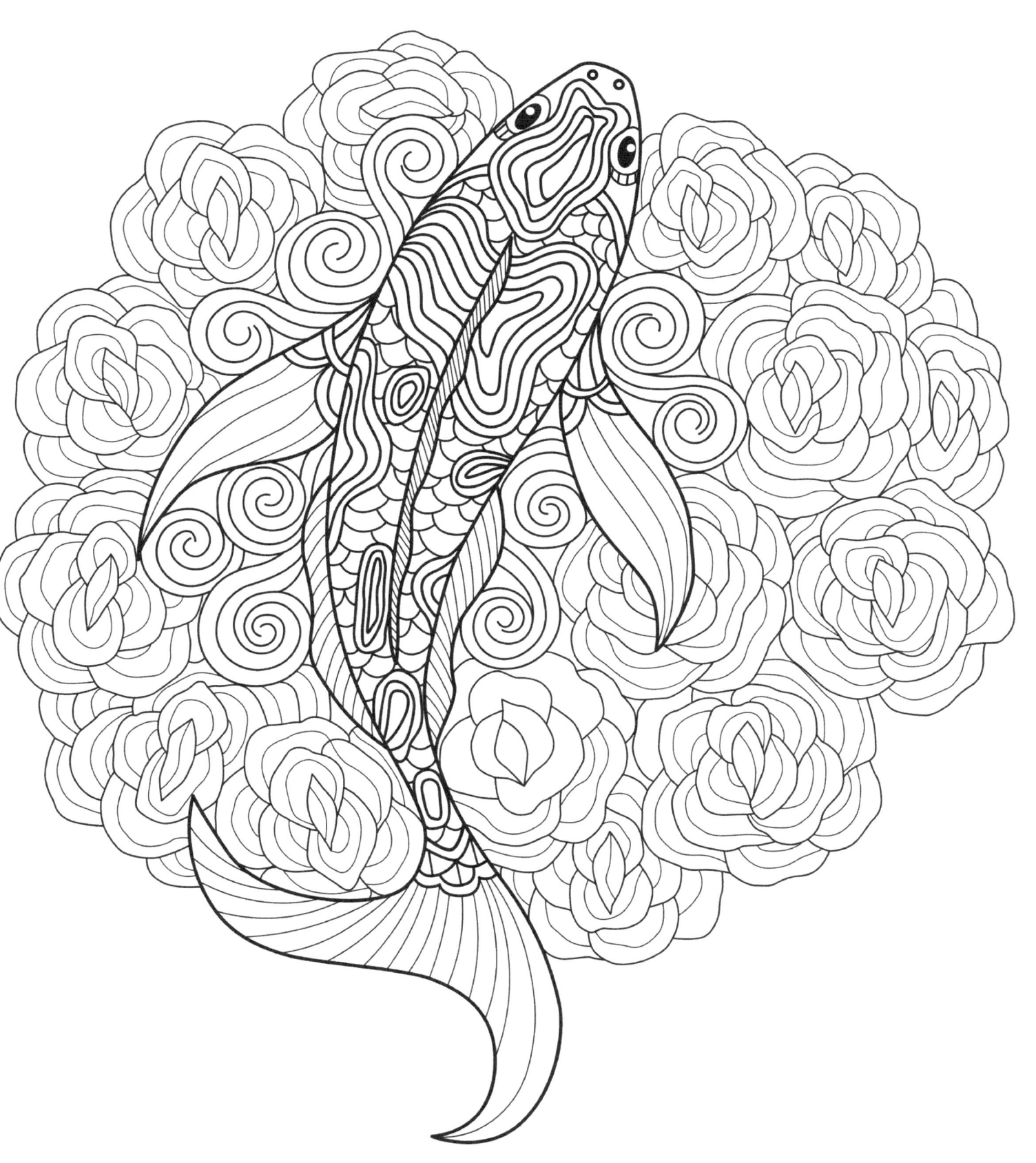

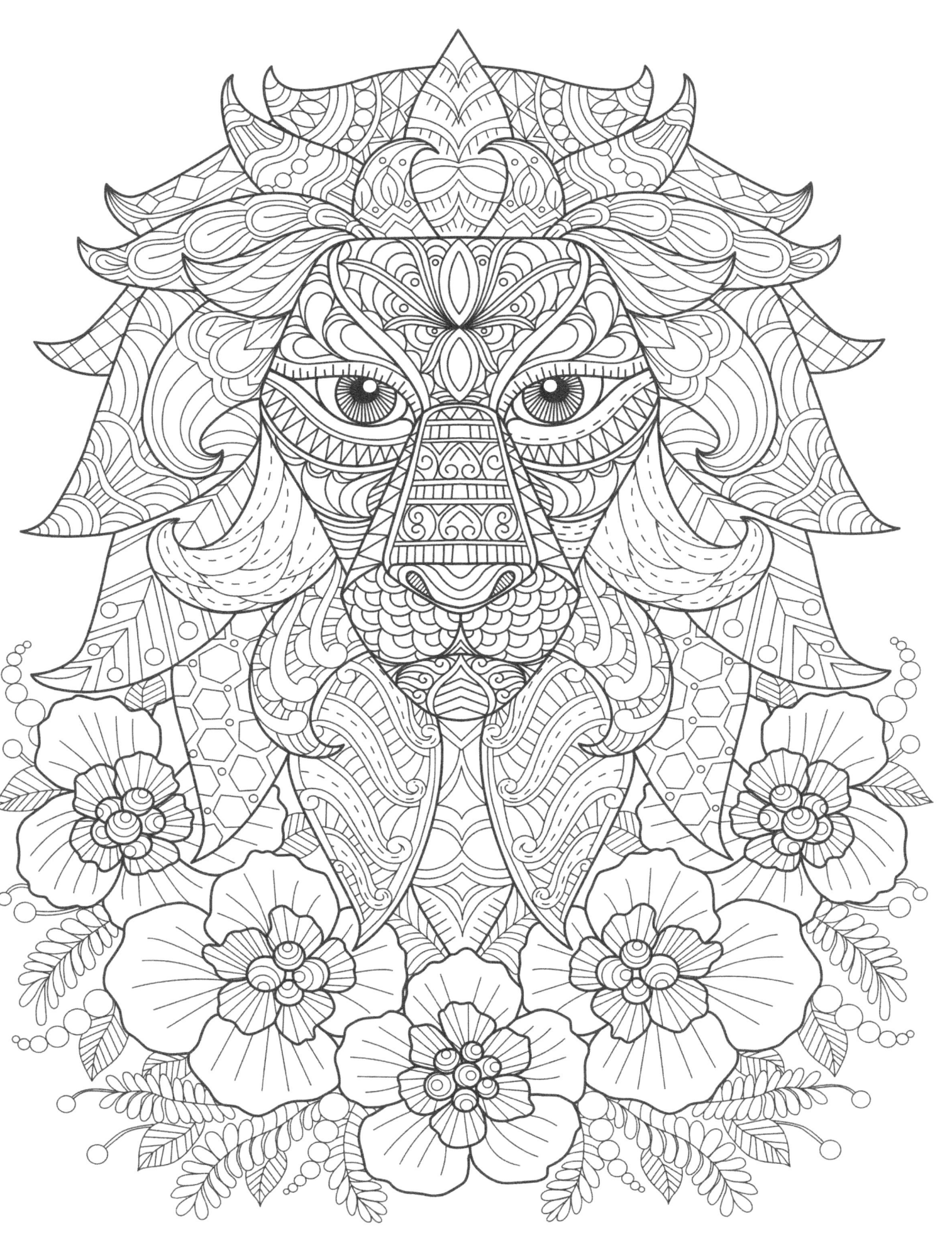

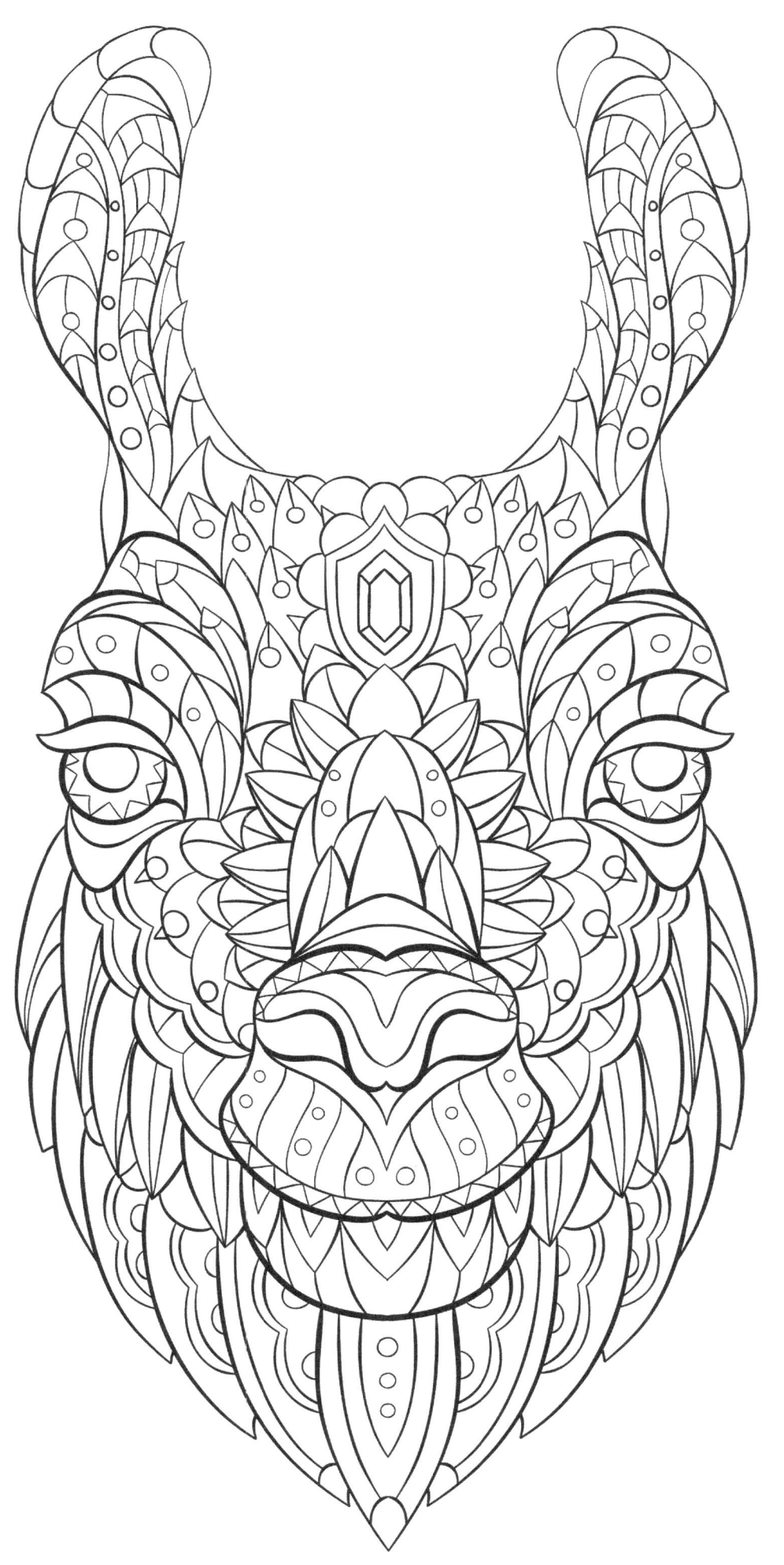

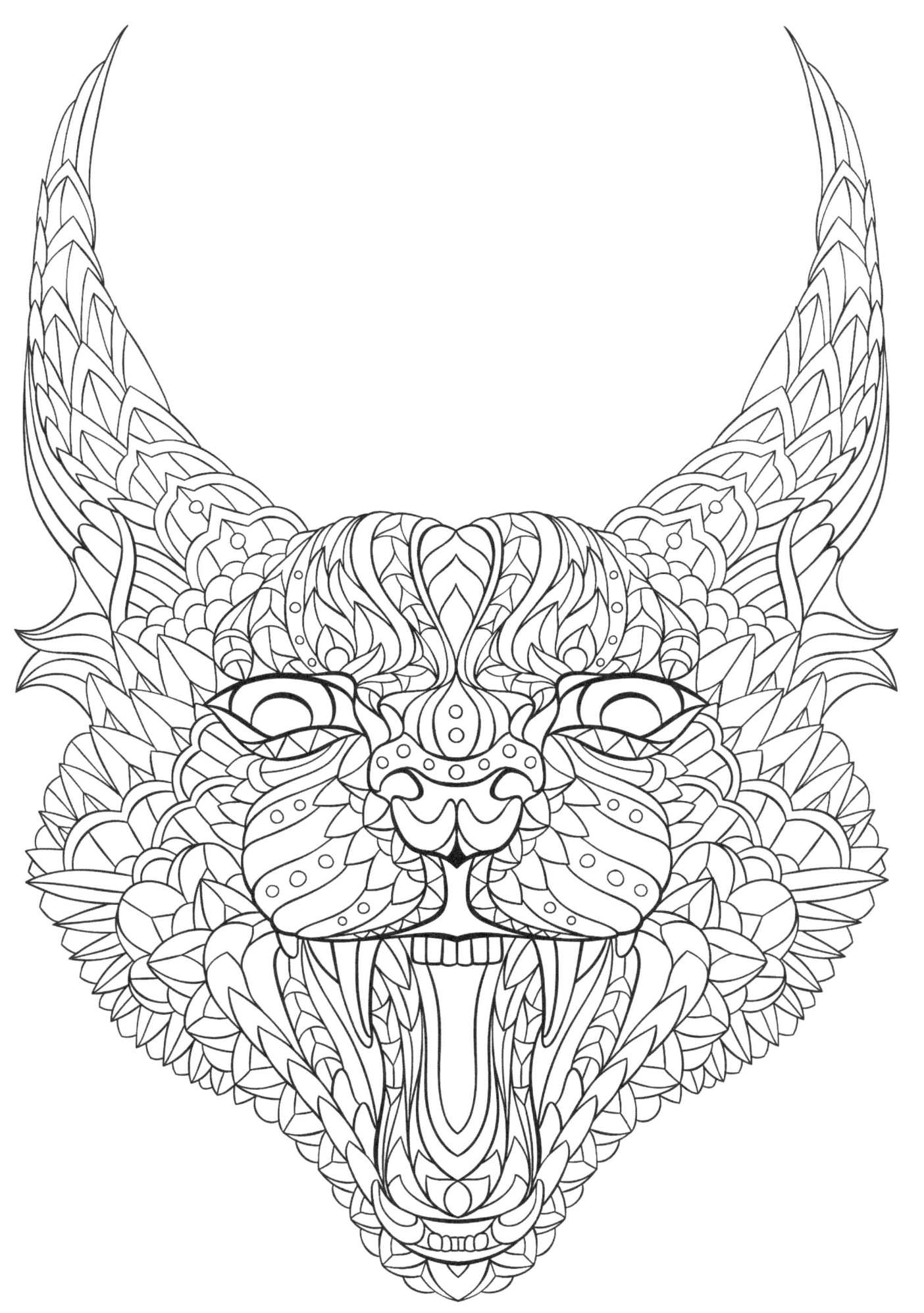

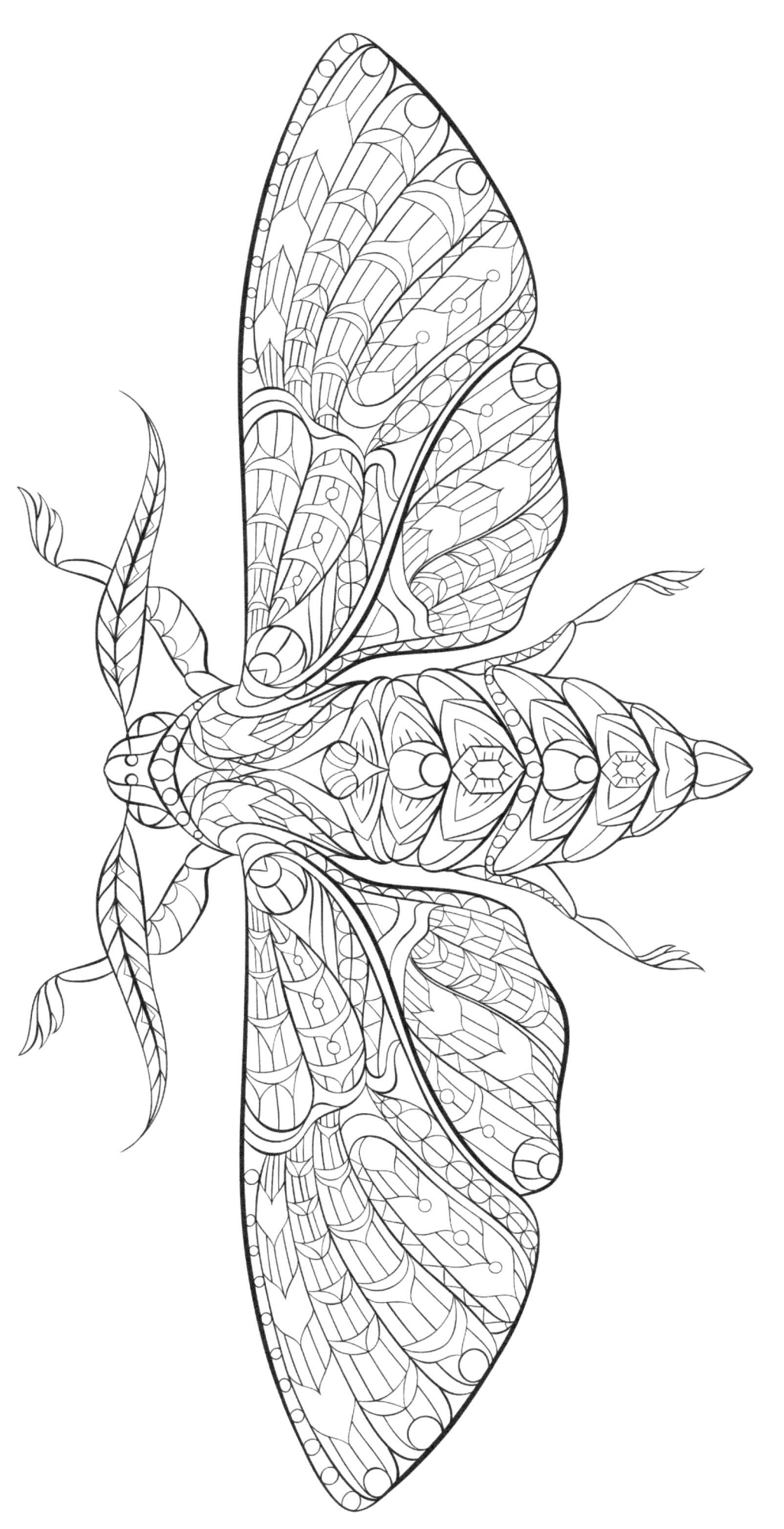

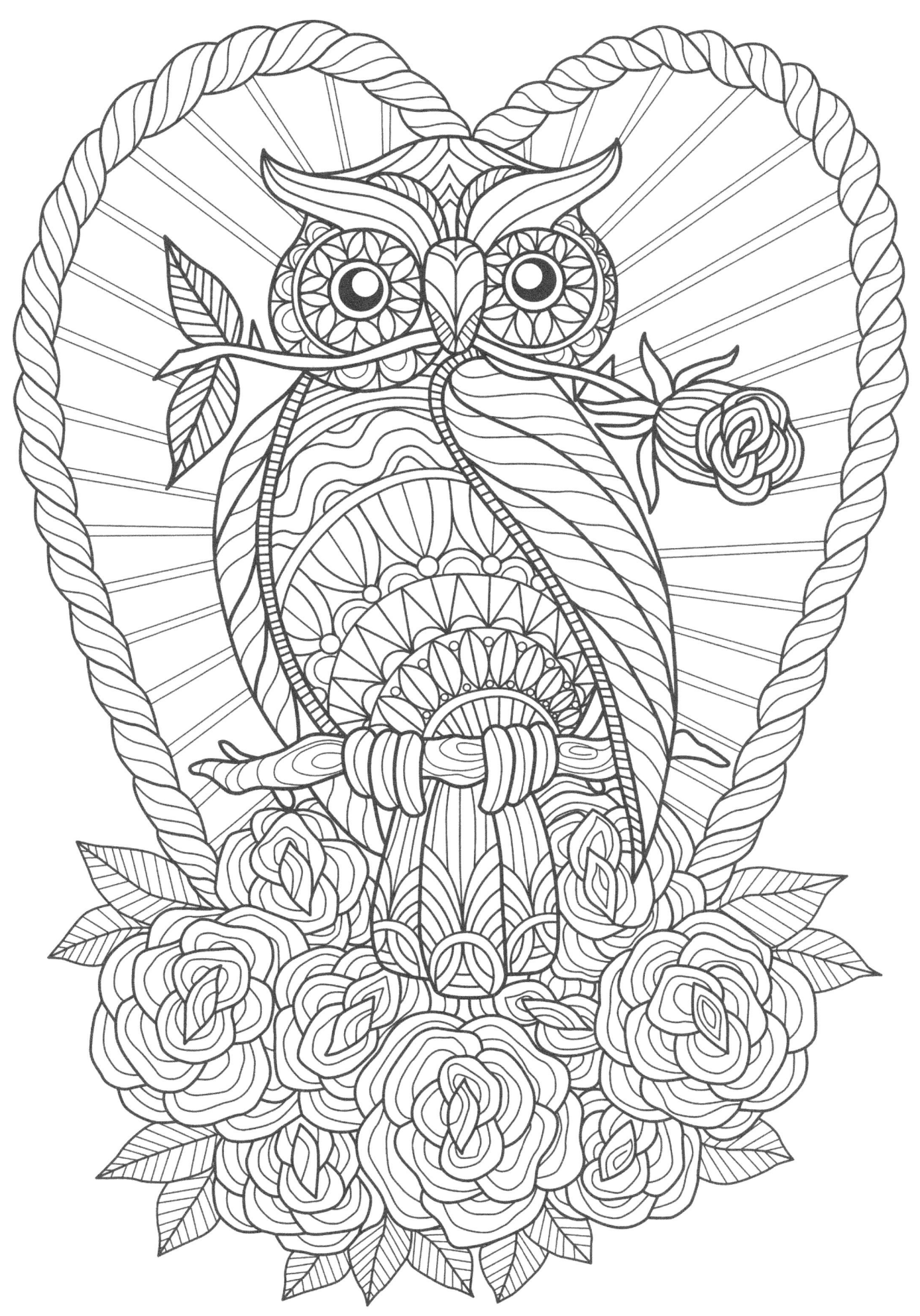

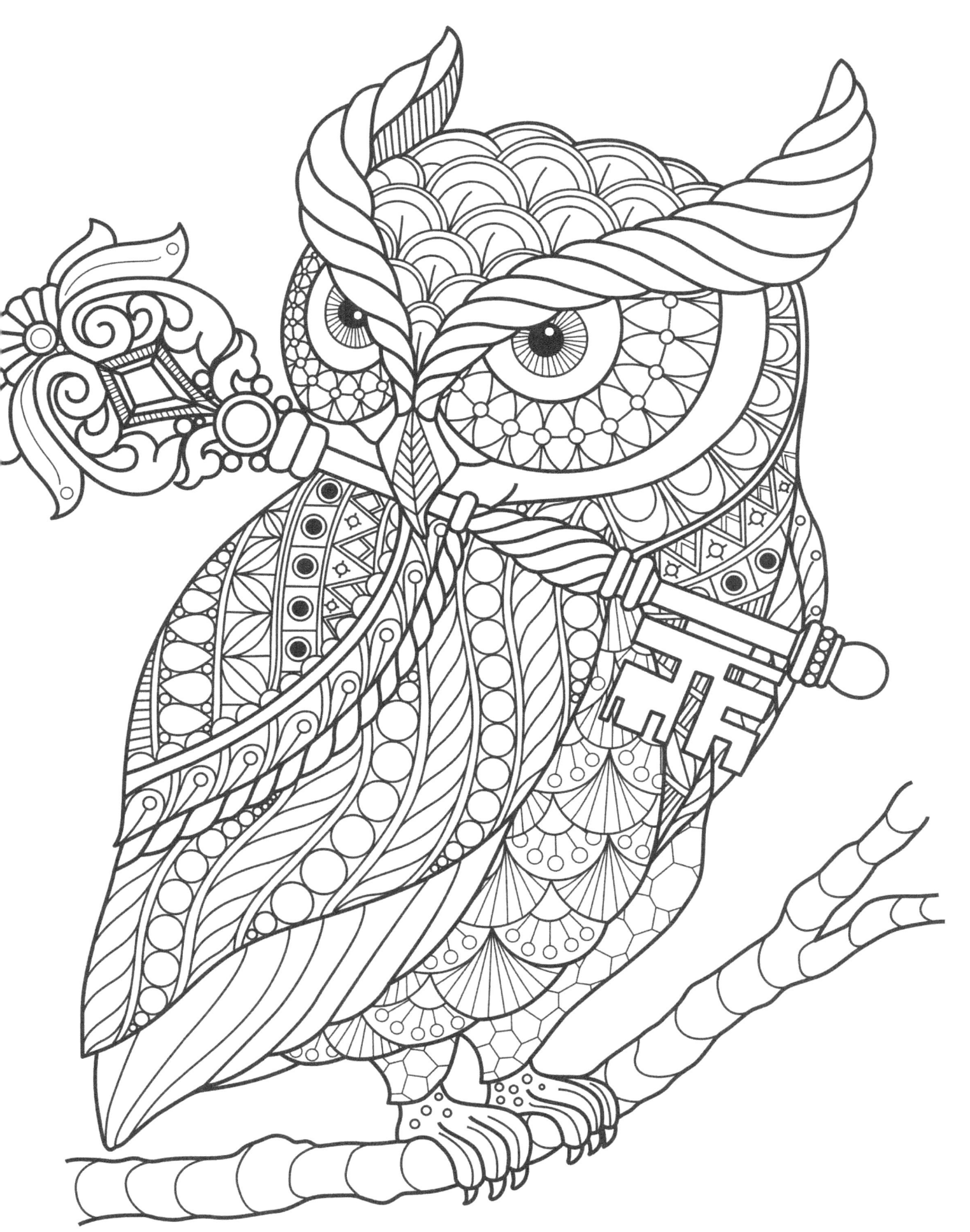

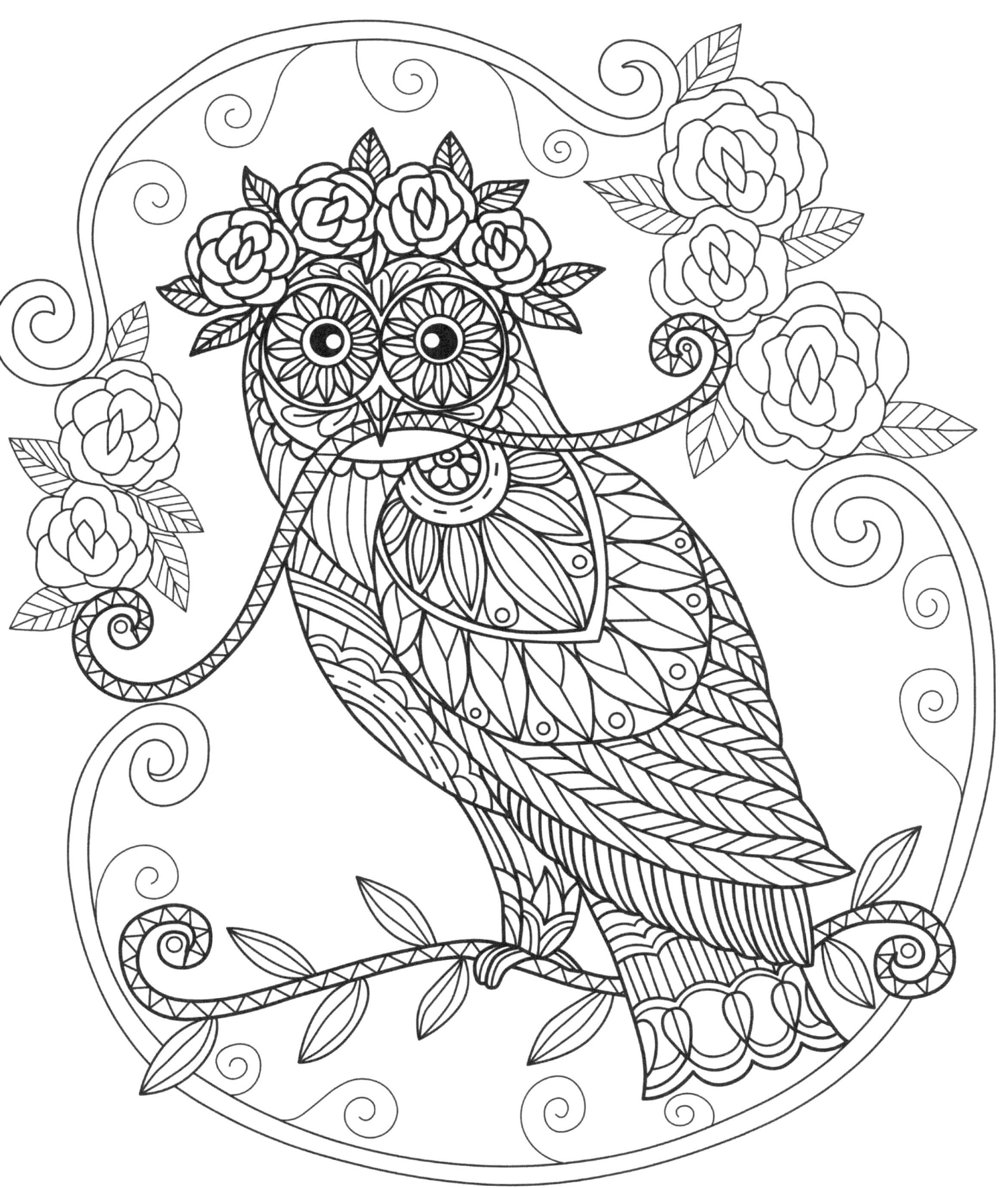

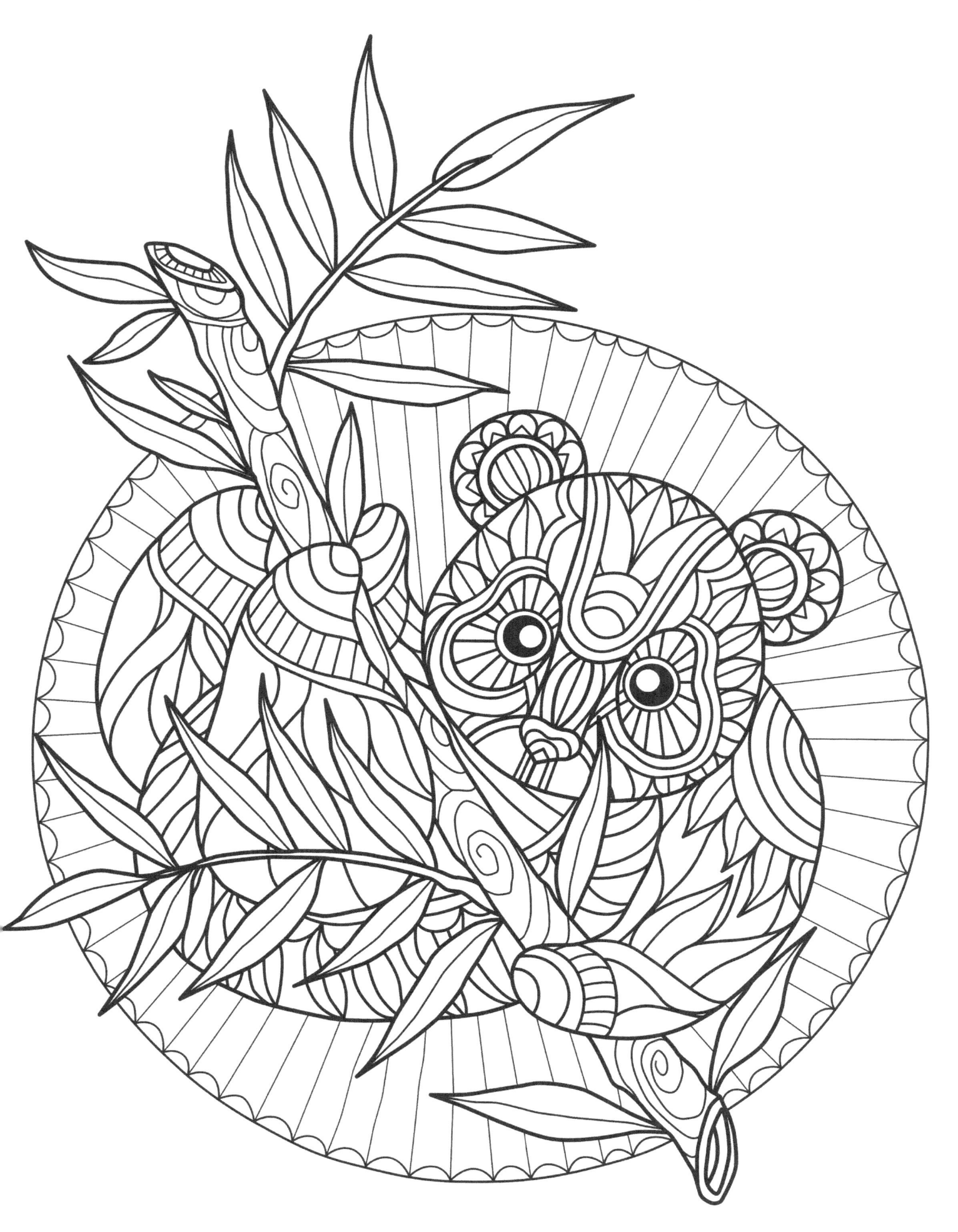

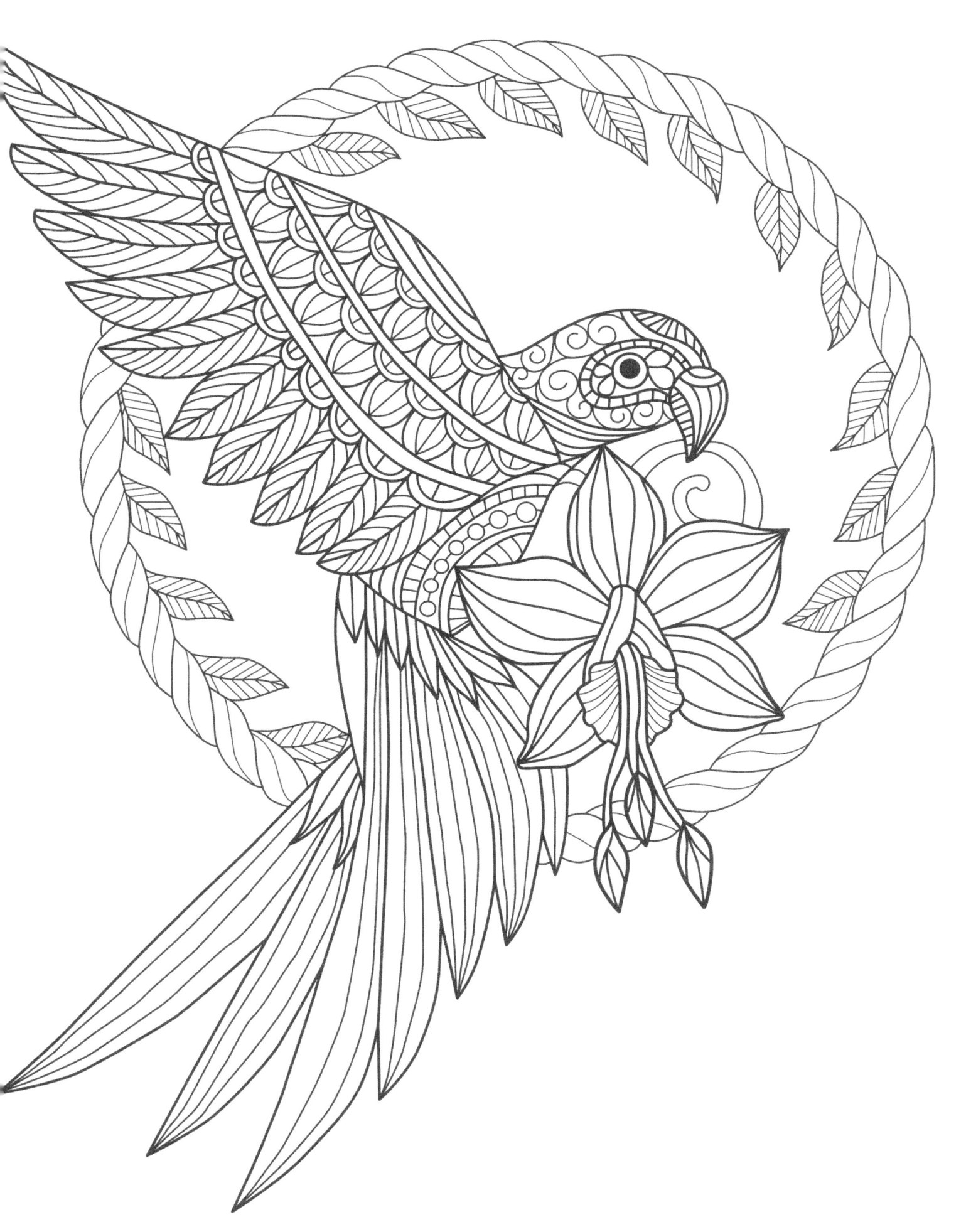

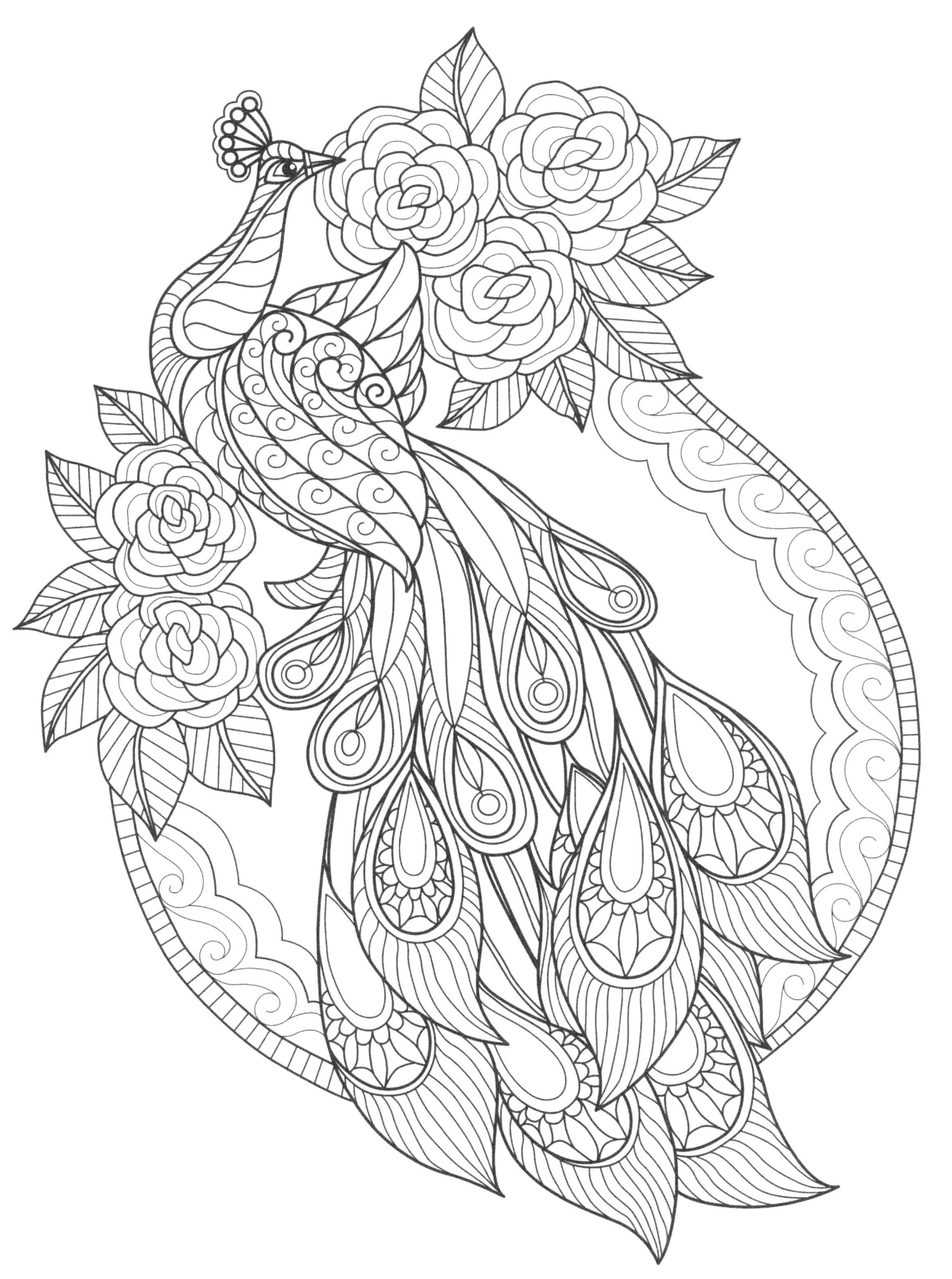

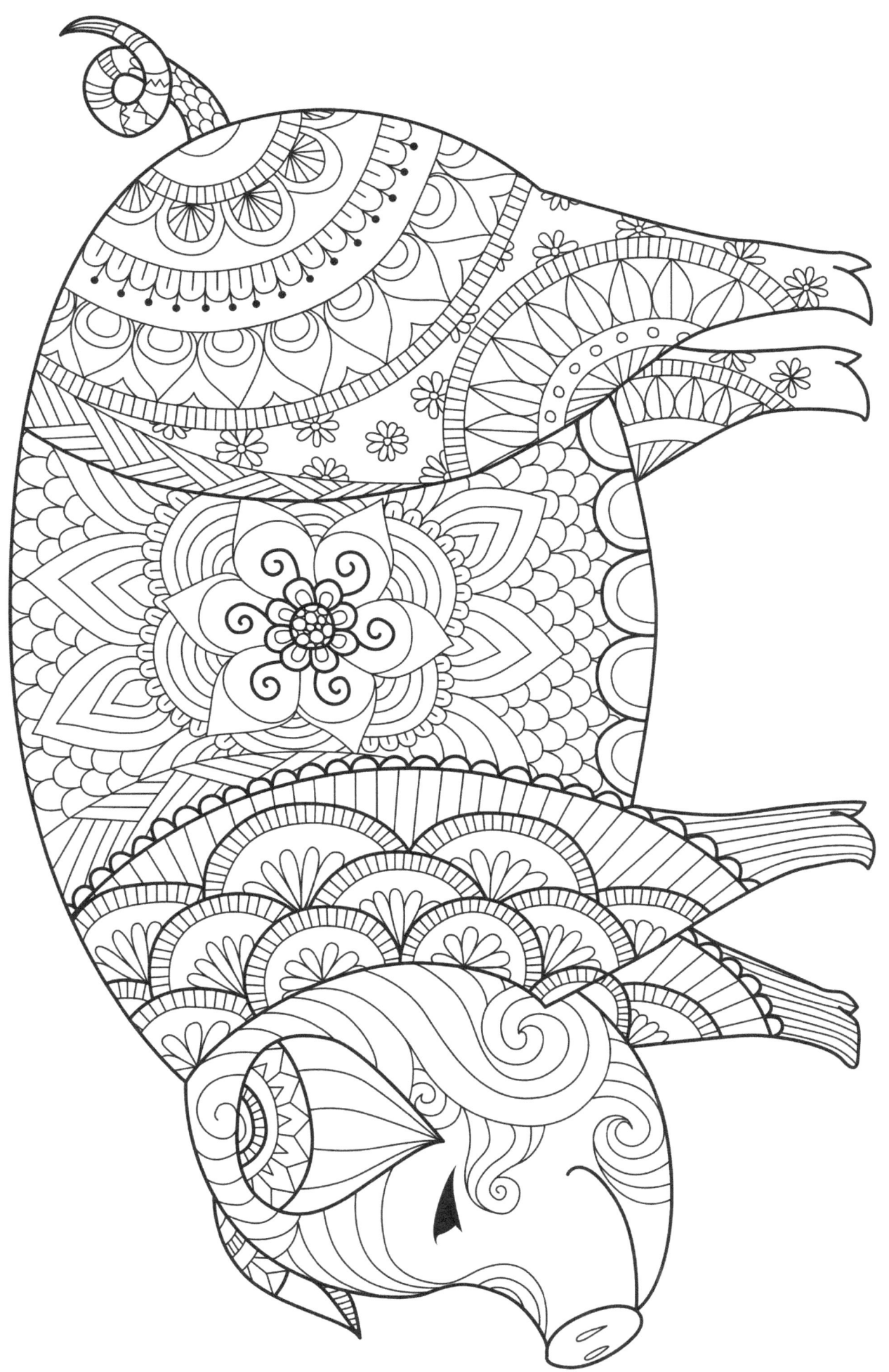

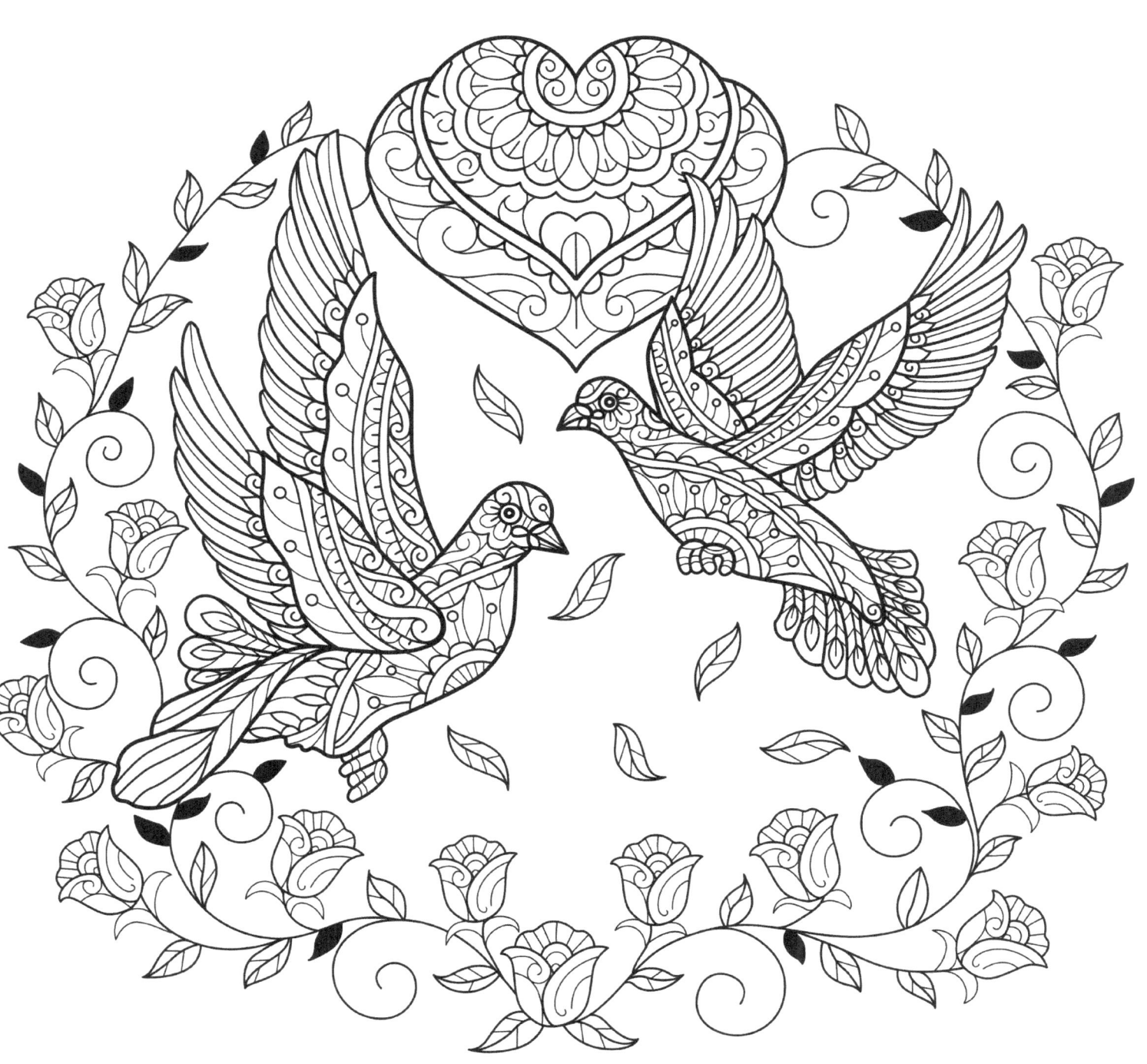

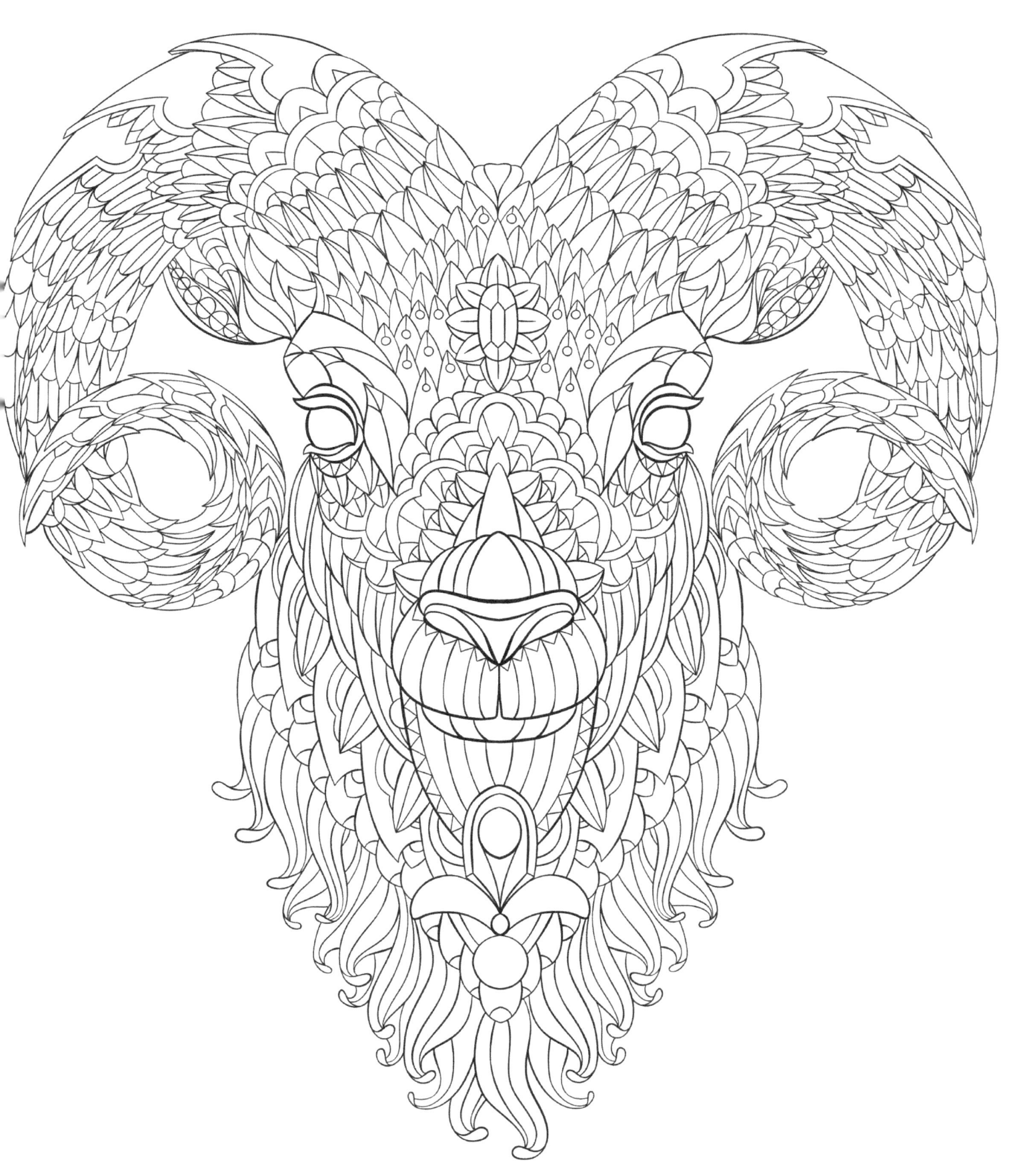

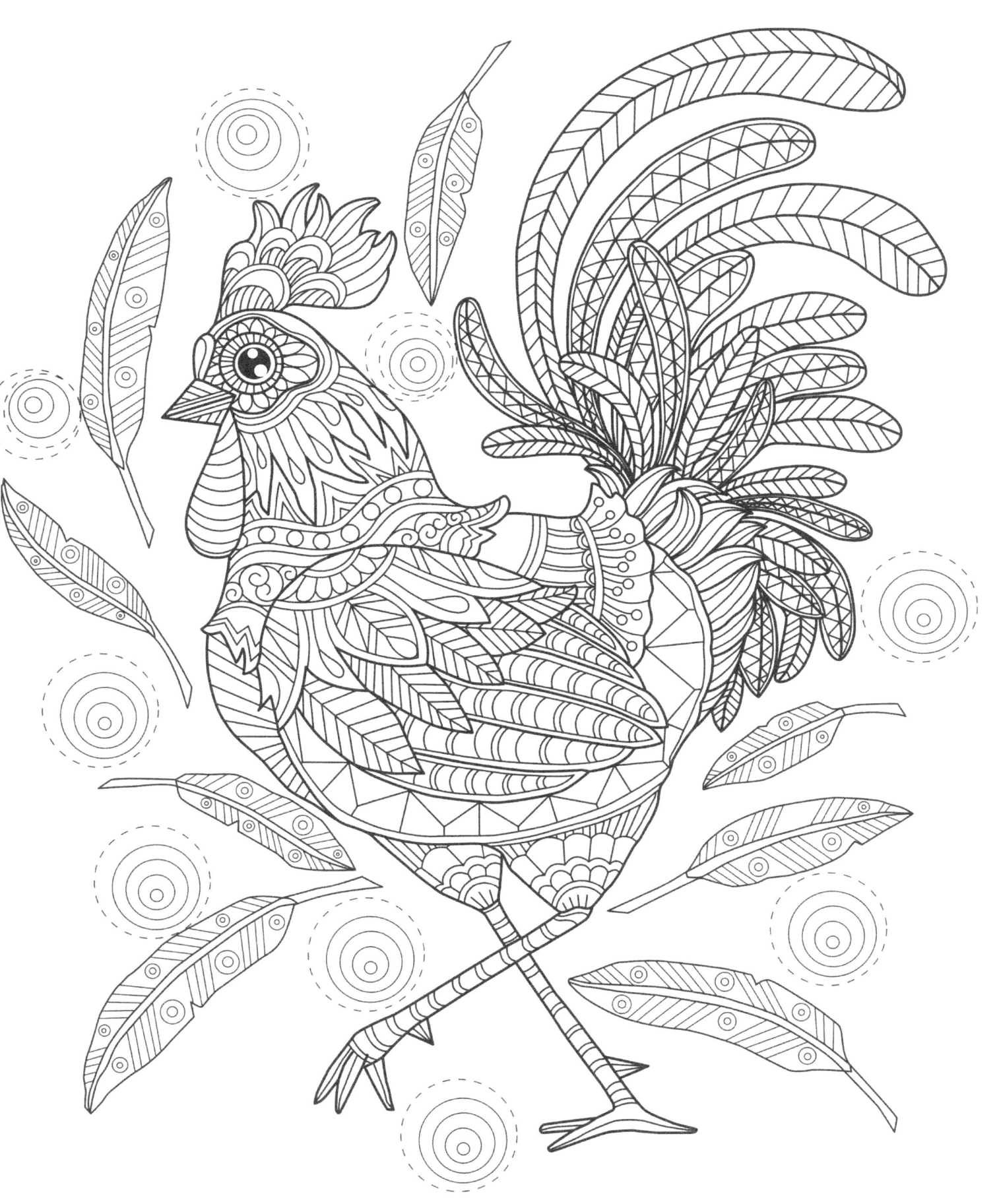

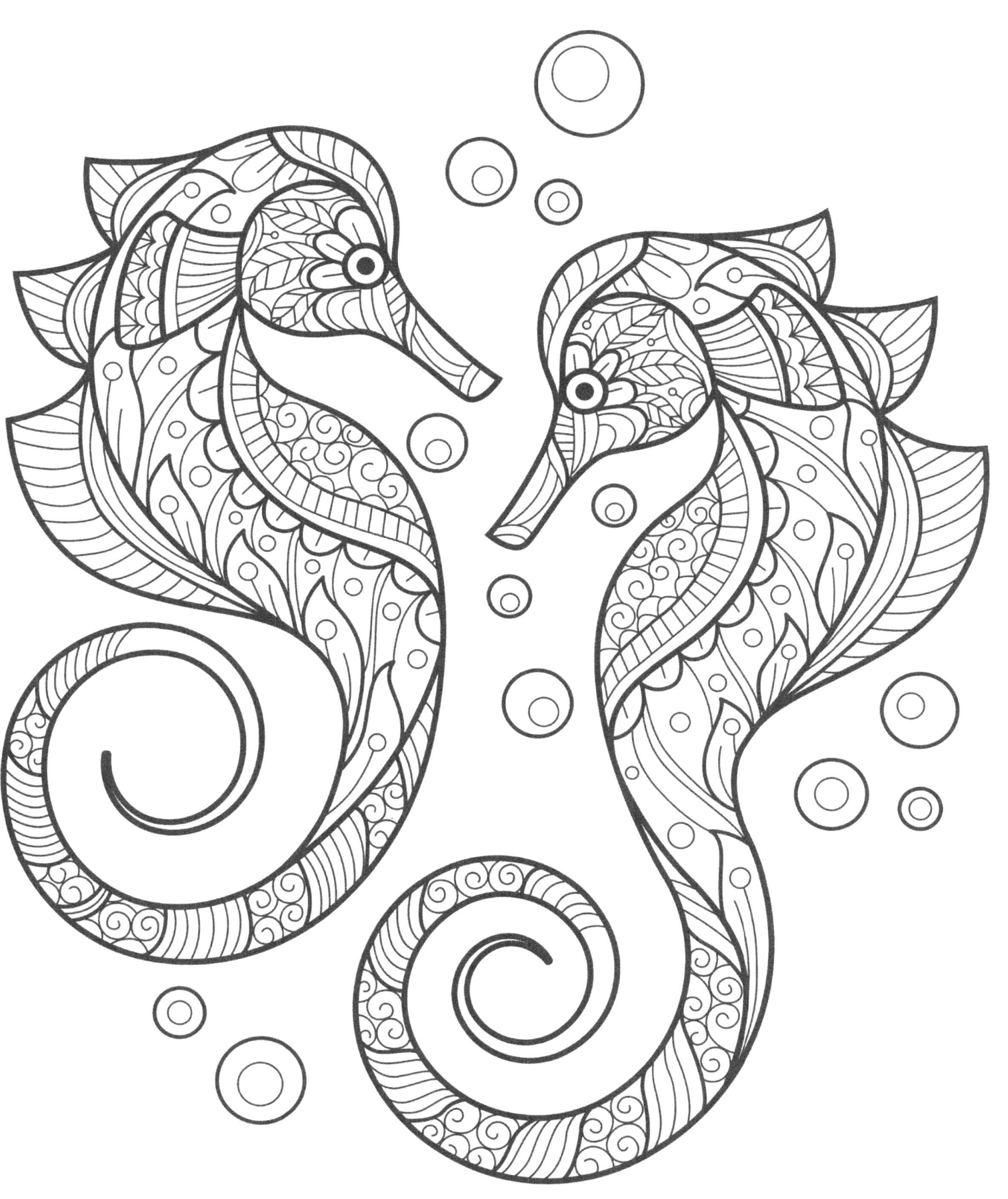

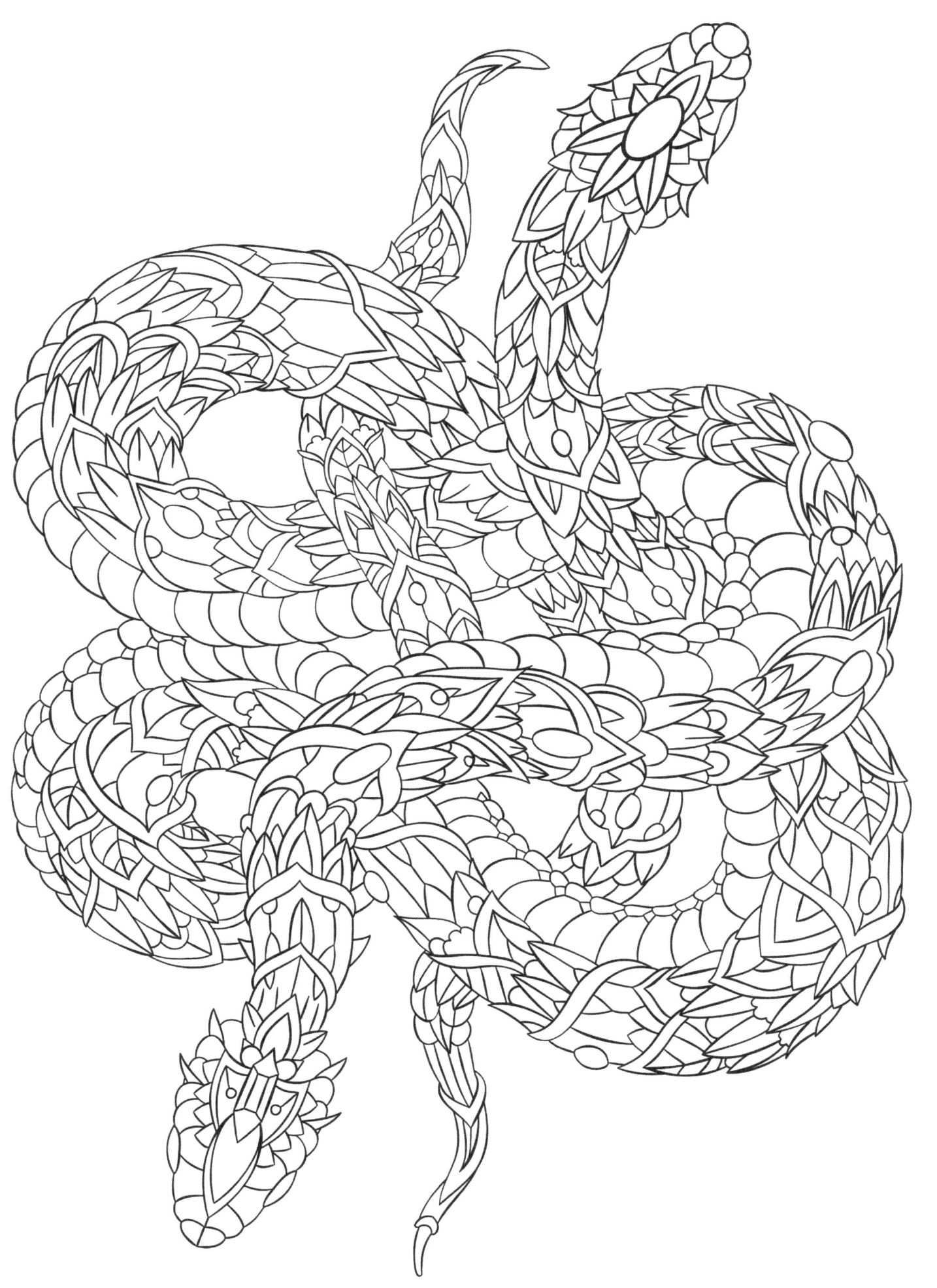

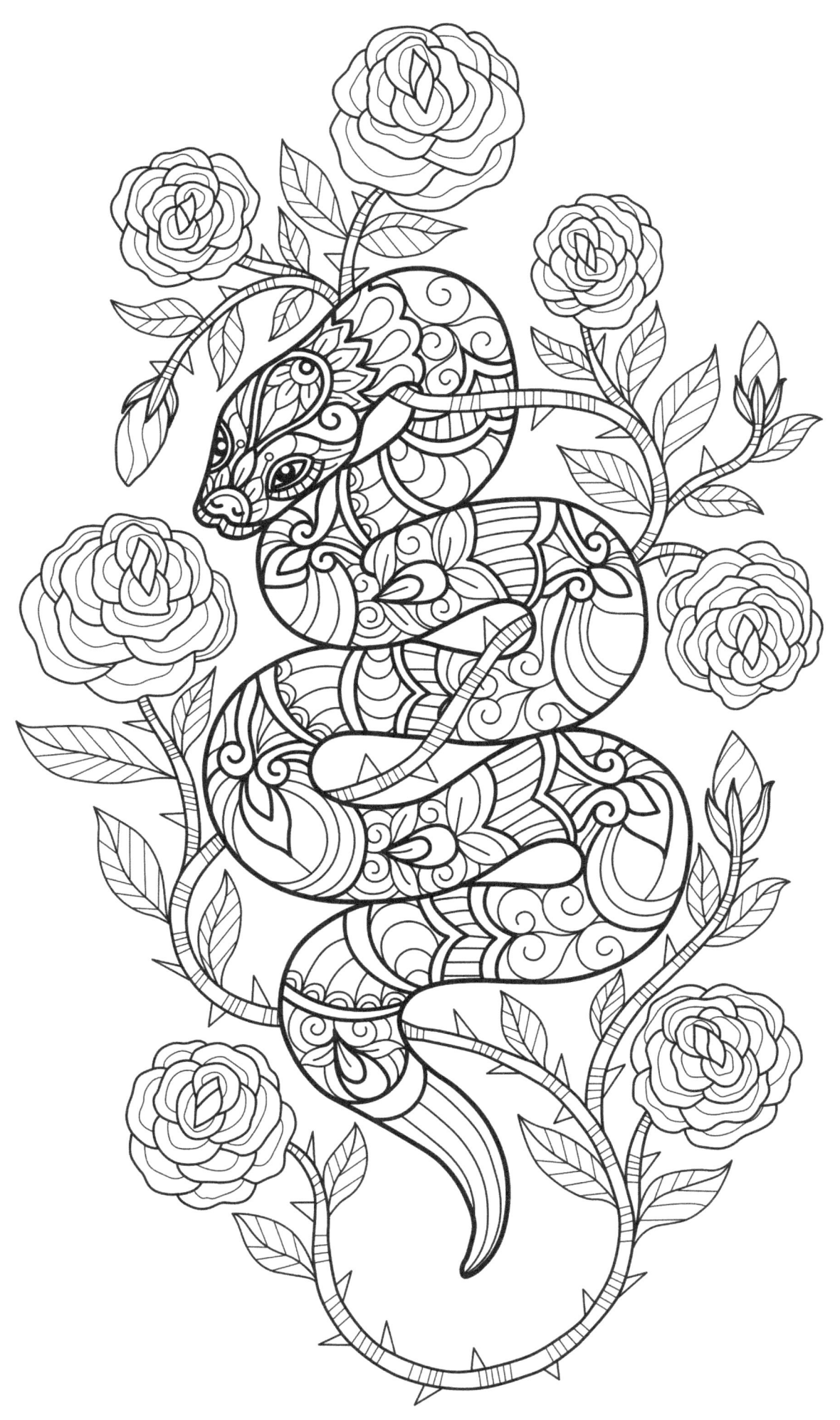

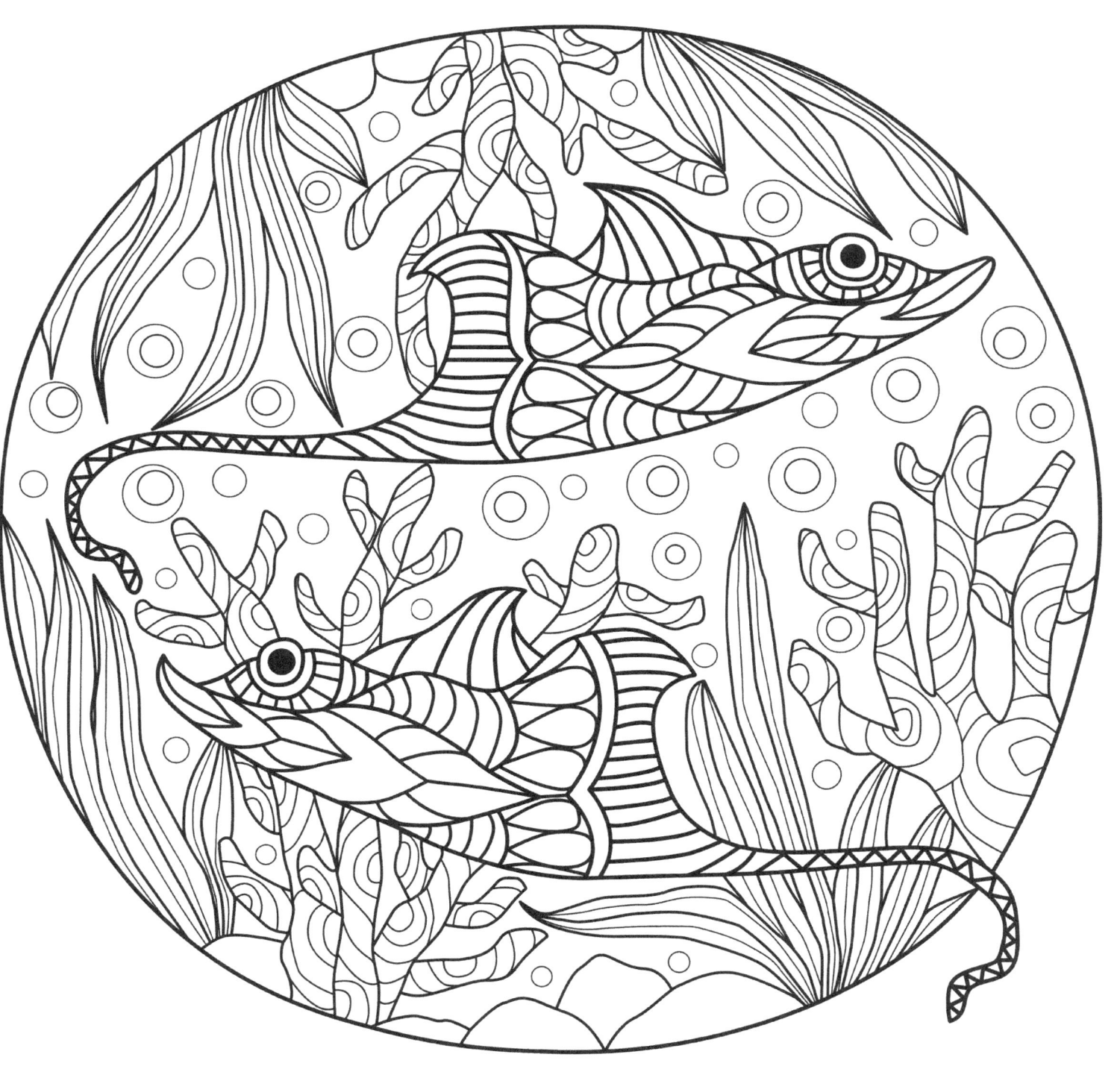

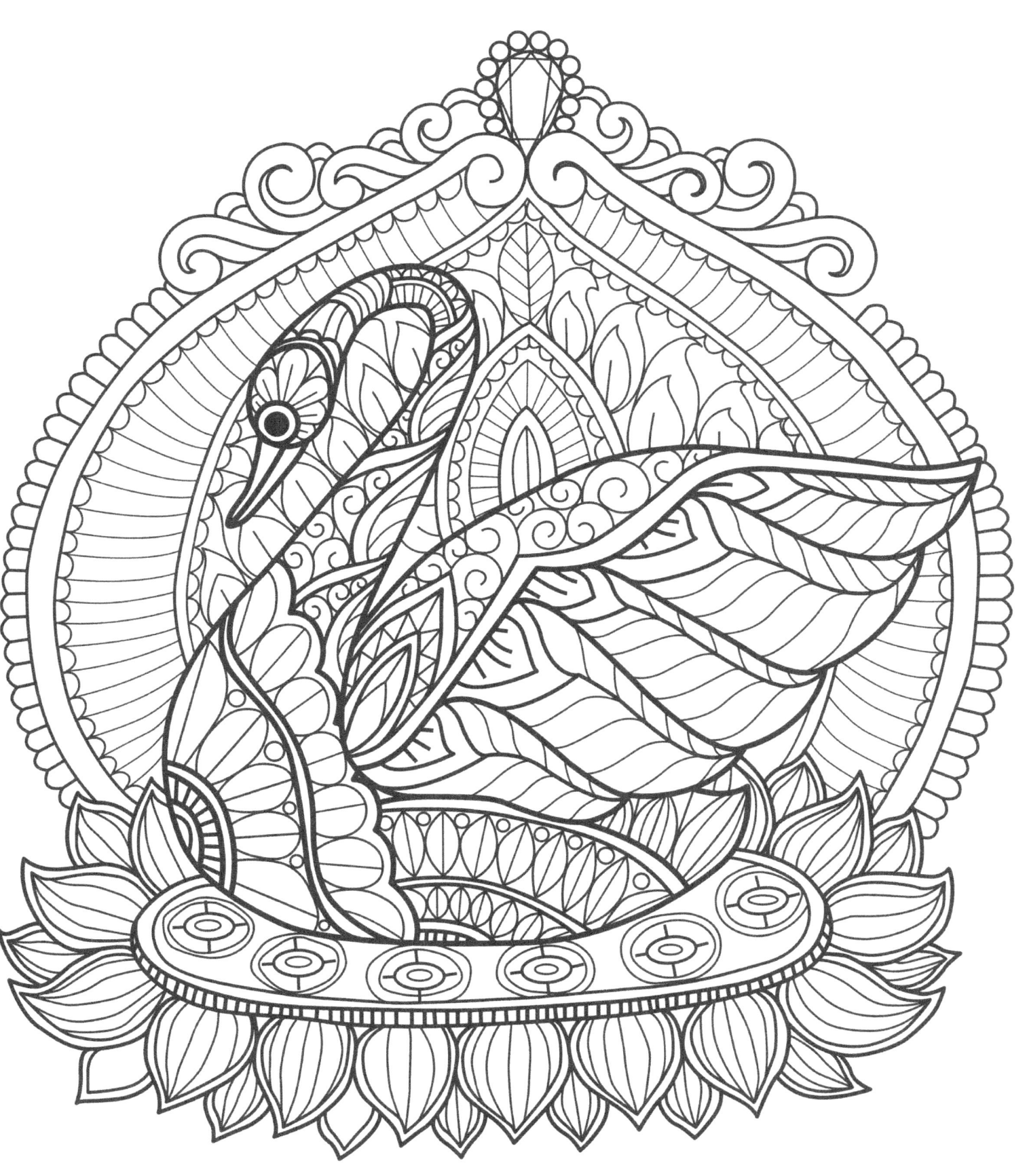

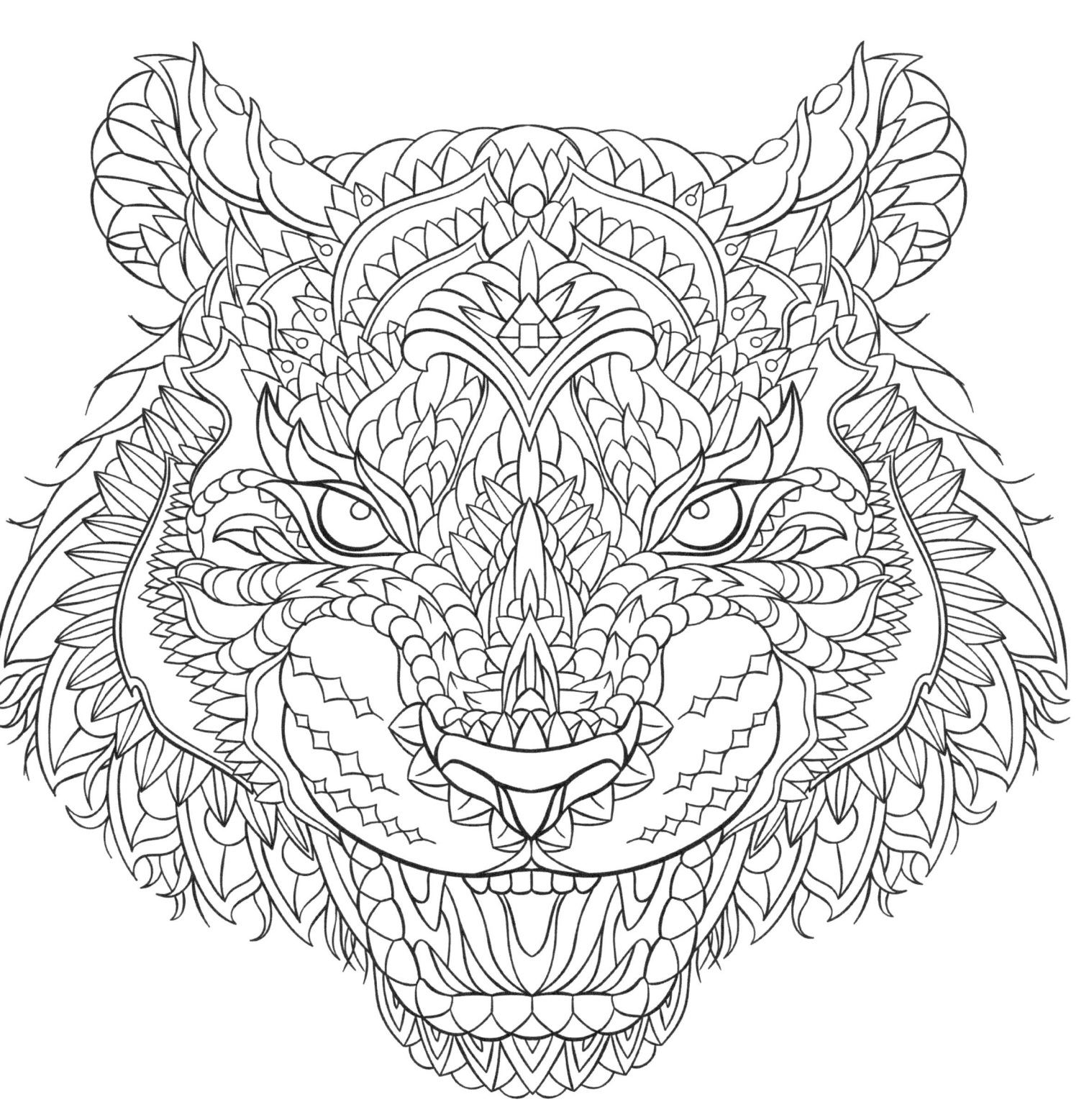

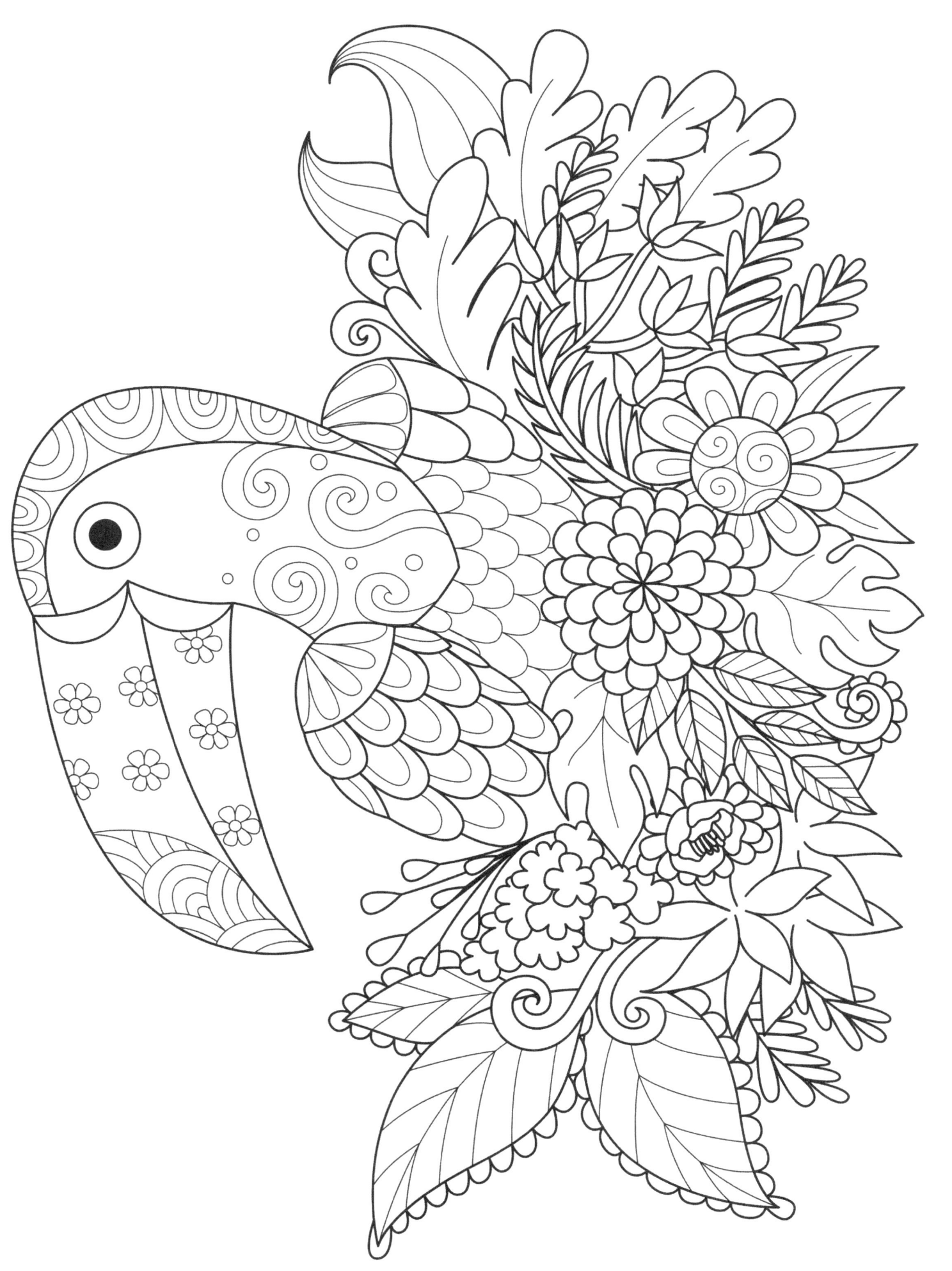

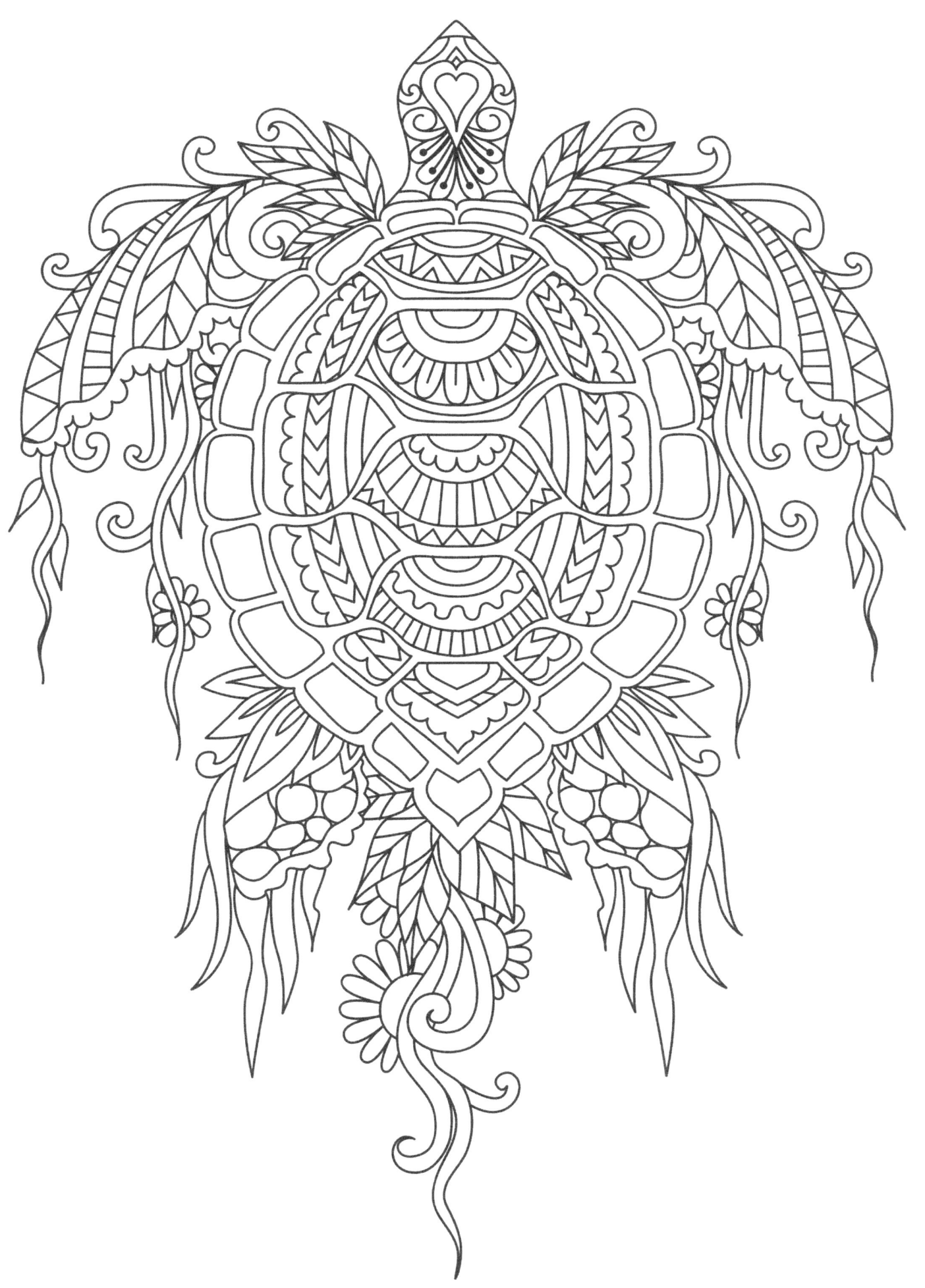

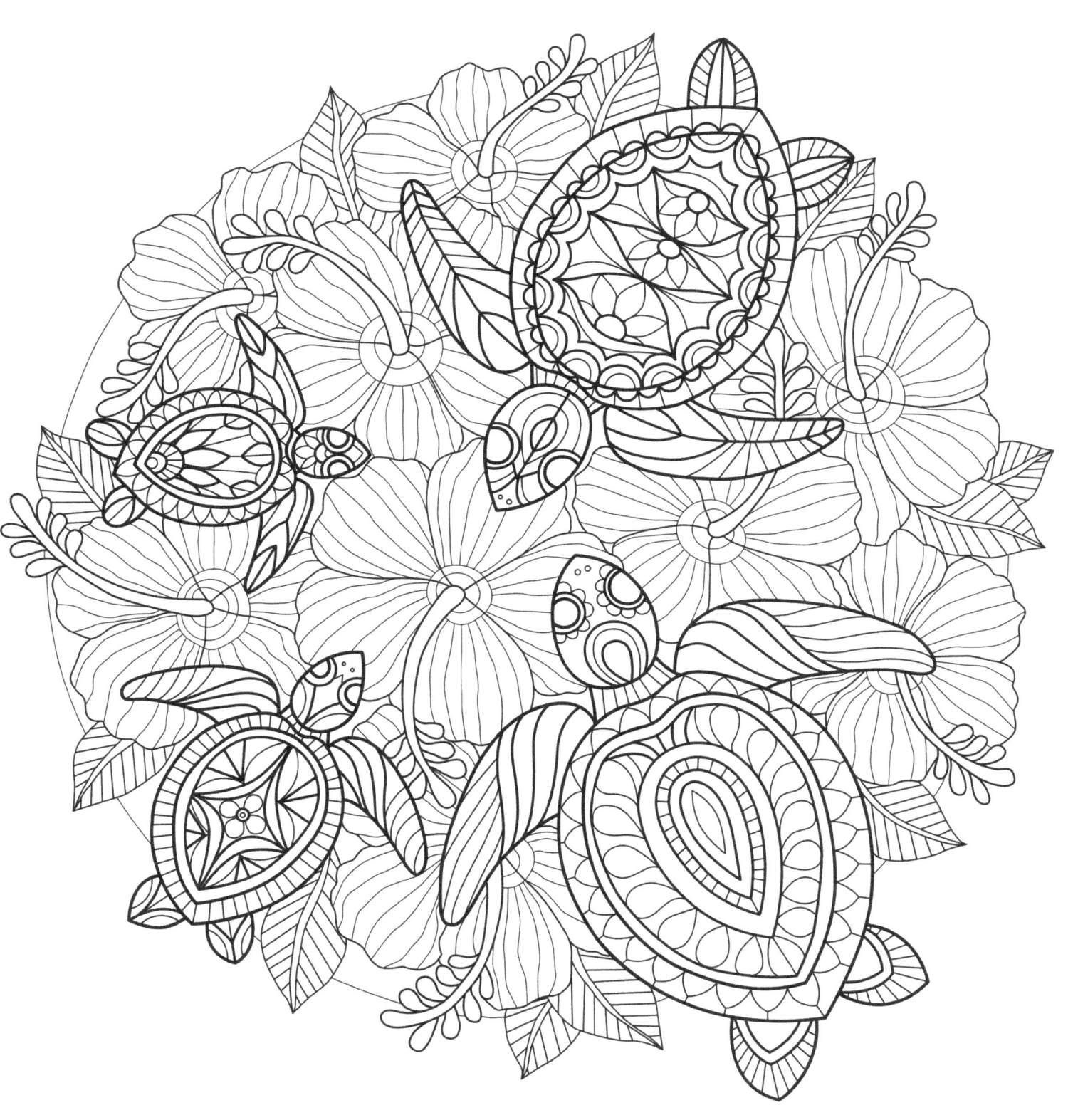

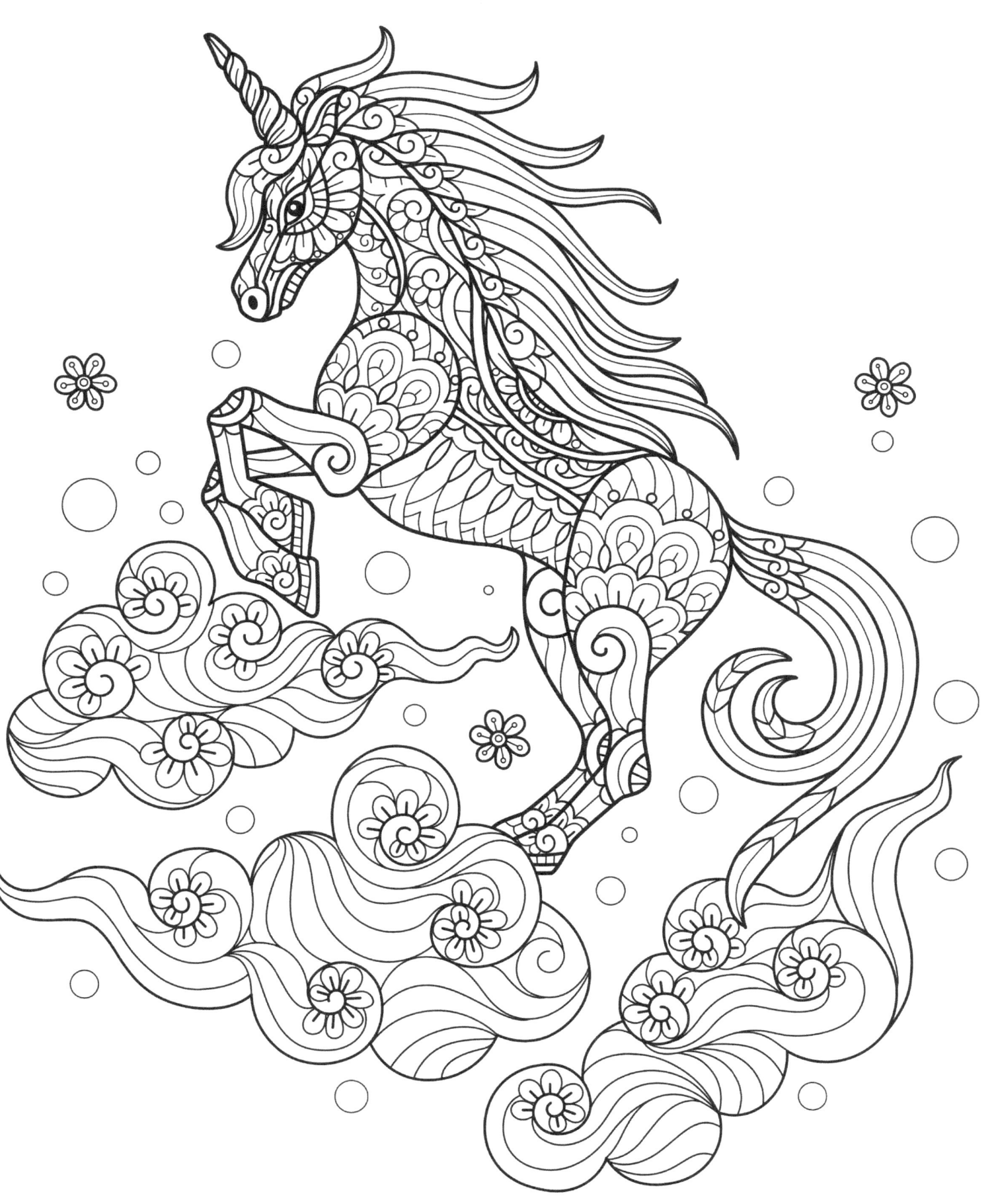

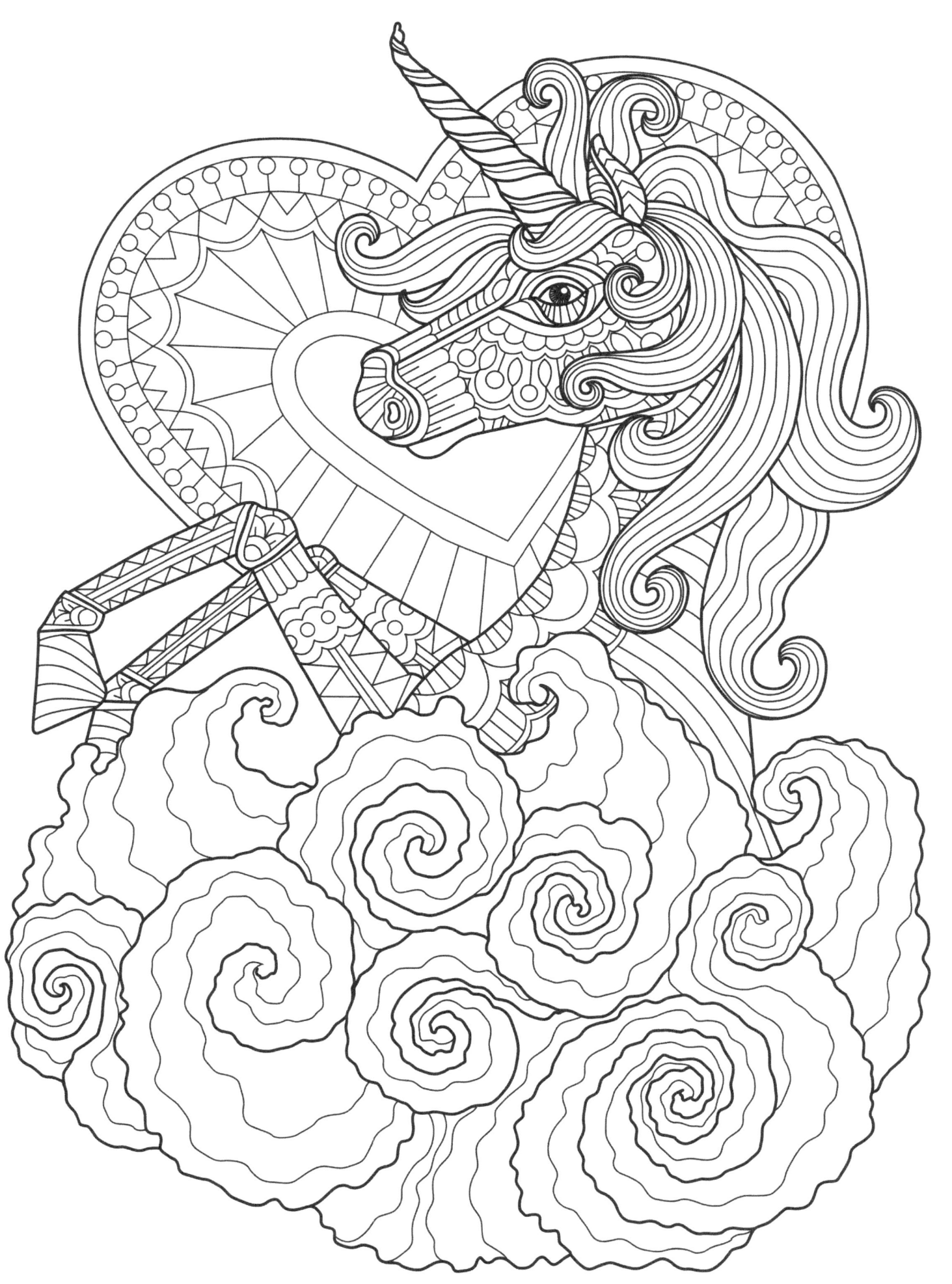

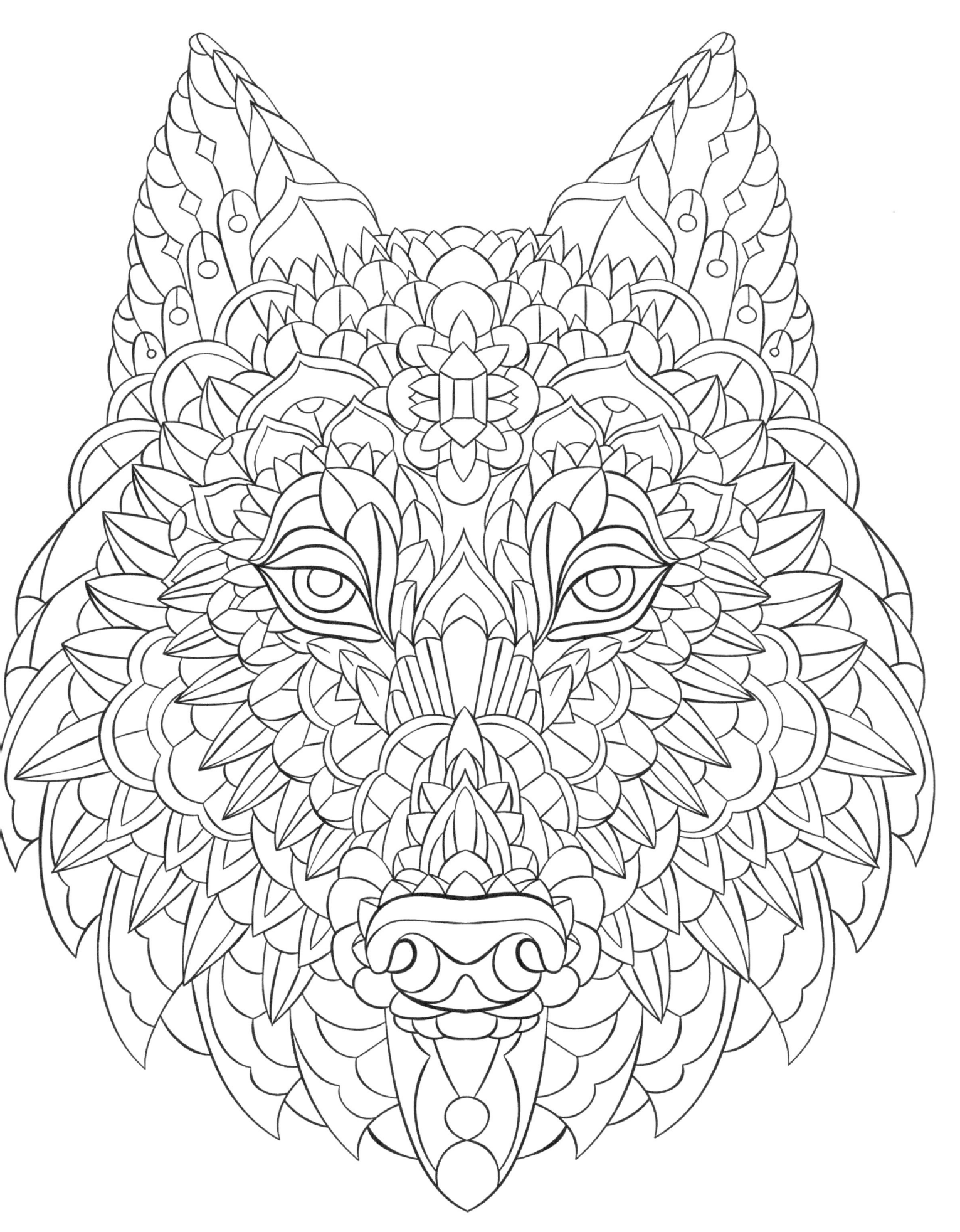

www.ingramcontent.com/pod-product-compliance
Lightning Source LLC
Chambersburg PA
CBHW080931220526
45465CB00008BA/3013